CRADLE OF ISLAM

HOW ISLAM BEGAN

DANIEL AMARI

RELIGION RESEARCH INSTITUTE PUBLICATION

Verses marked with Y. Ali are from Yusuf Ali Quran (English), translated by Abdullah Yusuf Ali. 1934, Public Domain.

Verses marked with Shakir are from Shakir Quran (English), translated by Muhammad Habib Shakir. Public Domain.

Table of Contents

Publisher's Introduction

The Religion Research Institute (RRI) has been researching Islam for more than 40 years. The conclusions of that research are published in multiple scholarly volumes that describe in detail its findings. However, it was always clear to our team members that there was a need for a simplified summary of these findings in popular language. This book, the "Cradle of Islam", is an attempt at such a text. With simple and concise language that paint the overall picture, the author managed to bring the summary of scholarly research to the popular level.

We hope our readers will become fully aware of the true motive behind this research. It was love that moved Dr. Amari to start studying Islam. Love that led him to spend decades praying for Muslims. Love towards Muslims. Dr. Amari had a very sincere desire to respectfully and reverently present to Muslims the vast wealth of knowledge he has uncovered during years of tedious research. Such knowledge will allow Muslims to be better informed and more aware of the vast history that shaped the faith they were handed since early childhood by their families and communities.

Author's Introduction

My first book about Islam, *Dawn of Islam*, was written to be a shorter introduction to early Islam than the multiple volumes (totaling thousands of pages) by my father, Dr. Rafat Amari. Though shorter, however, *Dawn of Islam* still contained quite a few technical discussions, which served serious students of Islam well, but was beyond the grasp or technical interest of casual readers who wanted an even smaller, more accessible book on the origins of Islam. That's how this book, *Cradle of Islam*, came to be.

Keeping the two books separate will allow the *Dawn of Islam* to grow technically without diluting the focus and brevity of *Cradle of Islam*. Readers of the *Cradle of Islam* might decide at some point to consult *Dawn of Islam* for more in-depth critical analysis of the Quran and the backgrounds of Islam and advanced scholarly discussions on the deity of Islam, interaction with latest scholarship, and textual criticism of the Quran.

Perhaps the topic of most interest and relevance to laypersons is how Islam began. To answer the question *Why focus on early Islam instead of on what Muslims believe today?* I could not find a better answer than the one Dr. Amari gave in his introduction to the *Quran & History*:

> Investigating the history of how a religion arose is one of the most important tests in examining the credibility of its claims. Despite whatever claims and arguments, later proponents of the religion added to the founders' sayings to lend support to the founders' claims, the facts regarding the religion remain limited to the period in which the founder lived. Therefore, the most important guiding principles for examining his claims and evaluating his religion are these: Studying the life of the founder, analyzing the religious and social environment in which he lived, and investigating the sources upon which he depended in founding his religion.[1]

My intention for this book is to present an accurate and truthful picture of early Islam based on the data we have. I am convinced that there is no meaningful engagement with those of different religions without the truth. Therefore, this book seeks to present early Islam as accurately as possible based on the latest historical investigations. My aim is not to portray Islam as good or bad but to present a truthful and accurate historical analysis.

I am thankful to the Lord for His sovereignty. It is clear that His plans cannot be stashed in the box of human reasoning and experience. He is worthy to be trusted. May all glory be to Him alone. I am thankful to all of those who supported, encouraged, assisted, and prayed for me.

Daniel Amari

[1] Rafat Amari, *Quran & History* (Religion Research Institute, 2018), 9.

MUSLIMS, TEXTS, VERSIONS

Syria
Mesopotamia
Kufa
Damascus
Jerusalem
Jordan
Paran
Aqaba
Sinai
Tabuk
Hegra
Hijaz
Yathrib (Medina)
Egypt
Mecca
Ta'if
Yemen
Ethiopia

Muslims

There is a difference between the terms "Muslim" and "Islamic." Muslim refers to a person whose religion is Islam. A female Muslim is called a Muslima or a "Muslim woman." The term Islamic, on the other hand, refers to anything related to the religion of Islam that is not a person; for example, an Islamic book, an Islamic school, an Islamic doctrine, and so on.

The overwhelming majority of Muslims were born into their religion. The fact that a child is born in an Islamic family in any country of the world makes the child automatically a Muslim. A Muslim man can marry a non-Muslim woman, but a Muslim woman cannot marry a non-Muslim man. There are many reasons for this. According to Islam, the children born to mixed couples, e.g., a Muslim man and non-Muslim woman, are automatically Muslims. The growth of Islam in the world today comes rarely from conversion and mostly from population growth, which is the highest in the world.

There is a sociopolitical system in Islamic countries that guards the Islamic religion in these children. It consists of several tightly cooperative entities that work together to ensure that each child grows to be a loyal adherent of Islam. These institutions include the government, schools, religious clerics, society, and family. All of these sociopolitical entities teach the child the importance of blindly following Islam, portray other religions as corrupt, and paint any historical or scientific criticism of the Quran as crusaders' deep hatred directed at the child for being a Muslim.[2] As a result of this, the Muslim child grows to blindly accept everything that is taught about Islam, to never question, discuss, or doubt any element of Islam, and to see any historical criticism of Islam as a form of personal hatred against the child. A Muslim sees himself as part of the religion. Islam becomes his or her personal identity, similar to race, ethnicity, and gender.

Even in Western countries, that sociopolitical system is propagated through family and the clerical systems, often with the blessing of those Western countries that are invested in portraying themselves as tolerant and multicultural. In such western countries, the rule demanding the killing of Muslims who leave Islam is a real threat.

It is important to bear in mind that Muslims are human beings created in the image of God. They come from diverse backgrounds, and there is a cultural component in each of them. Every culture has its own strengths and weaknesses, and we must be very careful not to confuse those cultural strengths and weaknesses with Islam. Regrettably, many confuse being an Arab with being a Muslim. In fact, more than 80% of all Muslims are not Arabs.

[2] Mohammed Ibn Shahbah, *Al-Israiliyat wa al-Mawduat fi Kutub al-Tafsir* (Cairo: El-Sonna Bookshop, 1987), 5.

At the same time, there is a difference between a Muslim and the religion of Islam. Regrettably, this difference is seldomly made clear. When we discuss Islam, the Quran, or Mohammed in this book, we never imply that any individual Muslim acts accordingly, lives similarly, or is guilty of any problems we discuss. Only a minority of Muslims truly follow the texts of Islam. Islam today is not identical to early Islam.[3] This book is not about Muslims today but rather about the ideas and systems that gave rise to Islam in an era 1,400 years ago.

The Islamic clerics, however, serving their agendas are heavily invested in confusing the two categories *Islam* and *Muslims*. They do so to prevent critical examination of the system, texts, and worldview by presenting them all as a protected personal identity associated with humanity. They do this because, to them, people are only tools for their desires and furthering their interests. But any person, society, or institution that claims to love and respect Muslims *must* separate the religion of Islam from the human being who is a Muslim. Otherwise, they are no better than those clerics driven by a political agenda for personal gain.

There are many sects in Islam. The most common are the Sunni and the Shia. The primary difference between the sects is not theological but rather which group of clerics holds the religious authority over the people. Each clerical hierarchy has a system of dictators who cooperate with them. Although the

[3] Cf. The chapter on Versions.

clerics of different sects utilize different texts, they all agree with the main text of Islam, the Quran.

Texts of Islam

Quran

The Quran is the main and primary sacred text of Islam. Islam claims that the Quran contains the words of Allah, the Islamic deity. The Quran consists of verses, similar to the concept of verses in the Bible. The verses are organized in surahs, which are chapters or sections of the Quran. The Quran contains 114 surahs. Each surah is given a name that loosely reflects a common theme or word within the surah. The surahs are not organized chronologically or meaningfully but according to size. The Quran was not written during Mohammed's time but began to be written sometime after his death. Traditionally, the surahs of the Quran are classified as either Meccan, those that were revealed in Mecca, or Medinan, those that were revealed later in the city of Medina.

What about the historical reliability of the Quran? In short, the author of the Quran collapses history chronologically.[4] It seems that the author of the Quran is unaware of the differences between years, centuries, and millennia. He presents historical

[4] For a summary account, cf. Daniel Amari, *Dawn of Islam,* 157. For detailed treatment, cf. Rafat Amari, *Quran & History.*

characters who were separated by thousands of years as contemporaries of each other.

Furthermore, the Quran reduces the geography of the world to the Arabian peninsula and immediate surrounding nations, setting Mecca as the center of the ancient world. The Quran places people who lived thousands of miles away from each other in the same location; likewise, it places people who lived thousands of miles from Mecca in Mecca.

Finally, the Quran does not distinguish between myth and history. It takes all mythical characters, pagan historical figures, biblical figures, and even pagan deities and makes them all historical figures and in some cases, Muslim prophets.

One could say that reading the Quran is like reading the famous book of myths *Arabian Nights*. But there are two differences. First, the Quran presents its many myths as historical facts. And, more importantly, some of these myths are hurtful and cruel, especially those that reduce Jews and Christians to pigs and apes. Rafat Amari states:

> The other populations of the world buried the myths of their ancestors thousands of years ago. How much more then should these primitive and inhumane myths have been buried so that no one should speak positively of them today?[5]

[5] Rafat Amari, *Quran & History*, 488.

Hadith

The books of Hadith are collections of teachings attributed to Mohammed in which he interprets and applies the Quran verses, makes determinations or rulings for certain circumstances, or simply provides a narration or teaching. Why are these collections, along with other books, vital for understanding the Quran? Unlike the Bible, the Quranic verses do not have enough context to provide full meaning for the text. The surahs are not organized in a helpful fashion.

Furthermore, the verses are not organized according to topic or context. They resemble an ad hoc collection. Moreover, unlike the Bible, the Quran does not provide its own interpretation. The Old Testament contains the writings of the prophets that interpret the Torah, and the New Testament contains the epistles that interpret the gospels. There is nothing like this in the Quran. Hence, the Hadith and other books such as Sira and Tafsir are vital for understanding the Quran. Many of the fundamental practices of Islam, such as the daily five prayers, are found not in the Quran but in the Hadith.

It is not possible to be a consistent practicing Muslim without these additional books. Some Islamic countries require Muslims to adhere to some of these books. Some Muslims, however, insist that these other books are unnecessary. In doing so, they are inconsistent. The overwhelming majority of Muslims insist that the Quran orders Muslims to follow the teaching and example of Mohammed; thus, they are proponents of Hadith (sayings or words of Mohammed) and Sira (biography of Mohammed). Sira will be discussed in the following section.

To the Muslims who follow the Hadith and Sira, the books of Hadith are important and carry as much divine authority as the Quran. However, the same proponents are careful to point out that the Quran has higher status than Hadith. The point is that to be consistent, Muslims cannot claim that only the Quran is inerrant. Mohammed's teachings and practices need to be inerrant as well since the Quran requires Muslims to follow his teachings and practices. Now in Islamic countries dominated by a Sunni majority, one will have no problem with this argument because when Sunni Muslims dominate both society and politics, they can shield the Quran or Hadith from any criticism. In the West, however, many Muslims insist on following only the Quran because they find it difficult to defend the Hadith in an open society. The argument concerning Hadith changes depending on whether one is in the majority or the minority.

But do these additional books such as the Hadith provide sufficient, reliable, and accurate data to help interpret the Quran? The answer is a definite *no* for many reasons outside the scope of this book. There is, however, another category of Islamic books to help in that regard: Sira.

Sira

Sira are books of Mohammed's biography. The difference between Hadith and Sira is that the Hadith emphasizes the words of Mohammed, while the Sira emphasizes the life of Mohammed in some sort of chronological order. The books of Sira are considered third in order of sacredness after the Quran and the Hadith. The basic idea is that the Quran is the word of Allah, the Hadith is the words of Mohammed, and the Sira is the biography of Mohammed.

Contrast this with the New Testament, which contains the life of Jesus, the teachings of Jesus, the life of the apostles and their teachings, and interpretations of the Gospels. While different books were written separately, we can put them together because they attest to each other and were distributed together as early as the first century A.D. Perhaps the biggest problem for a non-Muslim reading the Quran is that they would expect that the life of Mohammed and his words would be included in the Quran. They would expect it to include the interpretation of his words and life. For a book such as the Quran that insists that it is clear, it is missing the fundamental framework for understanding it and instead relies on collections of books written hundreds of years after the death of Mohammed.

Tafsir

Tafsir means commentary in Arabic. The Tafsir is a large collection of books written to interpret the Quran. Examples of books of Tafsir include Tafsir al-Tabari (different from Tarikh al-Tabari), Tafsir Mujahid, Tafsir al-Saddi, and others. Sunni

Muslims have their own books and Shia Muslims have their own. These books were written hundreds of years after the death of Mohammed. The above-mentioned works are among the earliest. While these books are helpful, they exhibit the symptoms of having been written late. When reading their commentaries, one cannot help but sense the gap between the time of Mohammed and the authors' futile speculations. But why are these commentaries needed if Mohammed's teaching interpreted the Quran? The answer: because the Hadith and Sira are not enough. They do not explain the Quran adequately.

This contrasts with the Bible. The Old Testament contains within itself lengthy writings of the prophets that interpret the Torah. While the Torah is focused on the covenant between Yahweh and the people of Israel, the Torah contains not only the text of the covenant, but also the events leading to the covenant, or the life of Moses, as well as the story of who God is, who man is, and where the people of Israel came from. But that is not enough. The majority of the Old Testament contains the writings of prophets interpreting the Torah. This suggests that these Islamic works—Hadith, Sira, and Tafsir—are vital for constructing and defining the Islamic religion, despite the enormous problems with them.

Versions

If you ask an average Muslim living in the 21st century to give a detailed description of what Muslims believe today, you might get an answer like this:

> Muslims believe that Allah is the name of the transcendent deity that created the universe. He is the god of all of the ancient prophets from Adam to Mohammed. There is only one god and he is unitarian. He [they insist] is the same god of the Old Testament prophets.

Further, the average Muslim believes the following:

> Abraham and Ishmael were Muslims who built (or rebuilt) the temple of Kaaba in Mecca. Hagar and Ishmael lived in Mecca, and so did the Ishmaelites after them. The famous well of Zamzam in Mecca was the spring of water that the angel showed to Hagar to save Ishmael from death. Abraham and Ishmael founded a monotheistic religion there that was the foundation of the Islamic religion.

Abraham and Ishmael practiced the Islamic rituals such as the great Hajj, or small Hajj (Umrah), Ramadan, and others. Abraham was described as Hanif[6] (plural Ahnaf). That group continued in Mecca until the days of Mohammed, who himself was a member of Ahnaf. Arabs came from Ishmael, and in particular Mohammed was from the progeny of Ishmael.

Mohammed was the last prophet of Allah. He was inspired by Allah through the angel Jibril (Gabriel) who gave him the Quran. He initially called Quraysh, the tribe living in Mecca, to become Muslims, but they rejected and persecuted him. Mohmmed thus migrated to the city of Medina where he was accepted. The Jewish tribes, however, conspired against him and he responded by attacking them. He called all pagan tribes to become Muslims and fought against those that rejected his call. But non-pagan tribes such as Christian tribes were given the additional option of paying tribute to remain in their religion. According to this version, Mohammed conducted his life in integrity, honesty, and truth, becoming the model human and the guide for all humanity. The whole world is obligated to believe in Mohammed.

Muslims believe that Jesus was a prophet of Allah. He was a Muslim. He was not the son of God nor was he crucified. Rather, somebody else was crucified in his stead or at least it appeared as though he was crucified when in fact he was not. The Trinity is a false teaching.

[6] Hanif is a member of a Mecca-based local cult called Ahnaf, established in the late 6th century A.D. at the earliest.

The Quran is the perfect word of Allah. It is inerrant and perfect in every aspect. It is perfect in transmission and the final revelation of Allah. The same Quran today is the Quran that came to Mohammed. The Arabic of the Quran is written in superior rhyme without any mistakes. Its superior Arabic language is a miracle of Allah and a sign that it is true.

There are 5 important pillars of Islam:

- Islamic confession (Shahada)
- 5 daily Prayers (Salat)
- Giving Alms (Zakat)
- Fasting of Ramadan (Sawm)
- Pilgrimage to Mecca (Hajj)

Muslims believe that the Quran, along with the selective Hadith and Sira, endorses the theology described above. They believe that all the above beliefs and practices is the same version from the days of Mohammed till today.

They also believe that the Bible, both the Old Testament and the New Testament (Torah and Injil or Gospel, as they call them), reflect this theology as well. They insist that in the past they contained explicit and direct references to Mohammed as the prophet of Islam. The fact that the Bible does not support their claim is clear evidence, to them, that the Bible was corrupted.

Much can be said about all of this, but I will make two comments here. First, the Quran does not speak of this corruption of the Bible, and in fact the kind of corruption required to make the Bible match the Quran is extreme. If one adds all biblical doctrines, teachings, narrations, events, and prophecies that contradict the Quranic account, they would add up to the majority of the Bible. Typically, the average Muslim does not have sophisticated arguments to offer on this. The typical argument runs like this: Since the Quran and the Bible disagree, and the Quran has not been corrupted and is the word of Allah, therefore the Bible has to be corrupted.

Second, what Mohammed worshipped is not identical to what Muslims worship today. There is a true divide between what Muslims believe today and what Muslims believed in the early 7th century A.D. How does one account for this discrepancy? I have chosen to use the term "version" in this book to differentiate between the two systems of belief. What Muslims believe today is one version of Islam, which is not identical to the version of Mohammed or even the version of the Quran.

I do not use the term version to refer to sects such as the Sunni and Shia. Furthermore, Muslims today strongly insist that there is only one version, and that their version is identical to Mohammed's and the Quran's. I will demonstrate, however, that this is not true.

Other Versions

There are many versions of Islam in the world. Most versions related to clerics are traditional but a few are more liberal. For example, a tiny but recently more vocal minority of Muslim clerics have presented a more liberal version of Islam. They try to create a version that is more modern, more compatible with modern science and history. They say that the Quran is inerrant only when it comes to spiritual matters. They try to divorce it as much as possible from the other Islamic texts. There are many problems with their attempts. Foremost is the fact that the discrepancies between the Quran and history cannot be resolved. Dr. Rafat Amari has written a comprehensive historical criticism of the Quran that shows that the Quran is a book that is utterly unreliable historically.[7] It questions the very essence of trustworthiness of the Quran even in spiritual matters. The fact of the matter is that Quran cannot be trusted in any claim that can be tested historically. If the Quran cannot be trusted in any such claims, then how can the Quran be trusted in spiritual matters, especially when they are built on an unhistorical foundation?

Dr. Rafat Amari's Version

Dr. Amari has presented a comprehensive treatment of early Islam. It is based on examining the data from history,

[7] Rafat Amari, *Quran & History*.

archaeology, religions before Islam, and the Islamic texts. Instead of focusing on one background of Islam, Dr. Amari subjected all backgrounds to consistent historical criteria to seek and present the truth. Furthermore, in Dr. Amari's work, there is recognition of historical elements within the Islamic tradition. These historical elements meet several historical criteria such as criteria of embarrassment, internal consistency, and external historical attestation. Therefore, certain elements of the Islamic framework need to be accepted, such as: Mohammed is a real historical person who was born in Mecca and eventually became the prophet of Islam, and most of the Quran was composed during his time. This balanced treatment of early Islamic history is driven by the goal of seeking the most accurate historical data about early Islam.

MOHAMMED

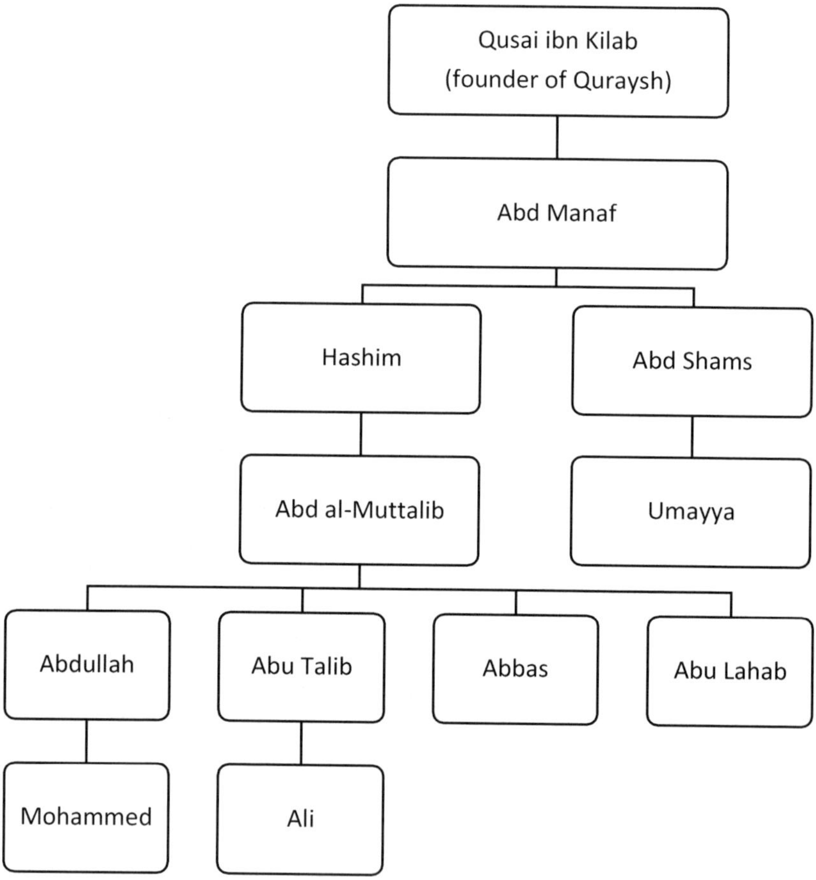
Qusai ibn Kilab
(founder of Quraysh)
Abd Manaf
Hashim
Abd Shams
Abd al-Muttalib
Umayya
Abdullah
Abu Talib
Abbas
Abu Lahab
Mohammed
Ali

Introduction to Mohammed

When discussing the life of Mohammed, how he came to be the prophet of Islam, and the beginnings of Islam, I have chosen to narrate the events from the perspective of those who exerted a major influence on Mohammed.

One challenging aspect of the study of the life of Mohammed is the names of the many characters who populate the story. They are difficult to remember, and they are many. This page (and a similar introductory page to the section on the spread of Islam) will serve as a quick reference to the various names and characters.

Abd Al-Muttalib	Grandfather of Mohammed. A pagan worshiper. He is famous for digging a water well in Mecca. He called the well Zamzam.
Amina	The mother of Mohammed. Also a priestess of Jinn.
Waraqa ibn Nofel	An important leader of a local pagan cult based in Mecca called Ahnaf.
Khadija	The first wife of Mohammed.
Aws & Khazraj	Two savage tribes living around the city of Yathrib
Abu Sufyan	A prominent leader of the tribe of Quraysh. Quraysh is based in the city of Mecca

Abd Al-Muttalib

Abd al-Muttalib was an important person in the history of Mecca. The city of Mecca is a small rest station on the land trade route built in the 4th century A.D. at the earliest. The city and the tribes were never known to be devoted to the God of the Bible. These tribes have no relation to Abraham or Ishmael, neither genealogically[8], nor in terms of faith and practice.

Mecca contained a temple called Kaaba built in the 5th century A.D. It was built by Asaad abu Karb,[9] a Himyarite leader, as a small pagan temple.[10] It was built in accordance with the pagan temples in Yemen and in accordance with the religious practices of Yemen.[11]

Abd al-Muttalib was the great grandson of Qusay ibn Kilab, the leader of the Arab tribe Quraysh. Qusay ibn Kilab was the leader who gathered an alliance of Yemeni families and attacked Mecca and took over this small city of Mecca. The alliance was

---

[8] For exhaustive discussion of this topic, Cf. *Islam in Light of History* by Dr. Rafat Amari. For a summary, Cf. *Dawn of Islam* by Daniel Amari.
[9] Dr. Rafat Amari suggested that the rule of Assad Abu Karb was during the time when Quraysh inhabited Mecca.
[10] Rafat Amari, *Islam in Light of History*, 386.
[11] Rafat Amari, *Islam in Light of History*, 250.

called Quraysh. Qusay ibn Kilab had two notable grandchildren, Hashim and Abd-Shams. Hashim was the grandfather of Abd al-Muttalib. Abd-Shams was the Father of Umayya from whom arose the Umayyad dynasty. They and all their descendants were pagans. The tribe was originally Yemenite, descendants of Noah's son Ham[12], not Shem.

Abd al-Muttalib lived from the very late 5th century[13] to the 6th century A.D. in Mecca. He was a very religious man, devoted to the syncretistic[14] religious system in Mecca. He was a worshipper of the stars and the idols that they represent. As a pagan, he named one of his sons Abdallah, the slave of Allah. The convention of this naming, slave of a deity or slave of a title for a deity, was very common in Mecca. For instance, you will find Abd Shams, slave of the sun, and Abdallat, slave of Allat.

Allah was a local pagan Arabian deity. He was part of the Arabic Star Religion. At that time, Allah was not the generic Arabic term for god. In fact, Christian Arabs before Islam did not use the term Allah for their deity.[15] Allah had a wife called Allat and daughters called Uzzah and Manat. There were important pagan rituals in Mecca and in Arabia in general to

[12] For exhaustive discussion, Cf. Dr. Rafat Amari's book *Islam in Light of History*.
[13] Late 5th century at the earliest. All traditional dates need to be taken with a grain of salt.
[14] Syncretistic indicates a mixture of multiple religions, sects, and ideologies.
[15] Daniel Amari, *Dawn of Islam* (Religion Research Institute, 2019), 195.

show devotion to these deities such as the various pilgrimages around Mecca or the fasting of Ramadan.[16]

Abd al-Muttalib had other children besides Abdallah: Abu Talib, the father of Ali; Abu Lahab, an enemy of Islam; and al-Abbas, the progenitor of the Abbasid dynasty. It is notable that from Qusay ibn Kilab came multiple dynasties that strongly shaped Islamic history. Note that the name Abu Talib means father of Talib; he literally had a son called Talib.

Abd al-Muttalib was also dedicated to the Jinn religion. In pre-Islamic Arabia, jinn were devils.[17] The Jinn religion of Arabia is an occultic religion centered around priestesses and priests, called kuhhan, who made contact with these jinn. These priestesses served as mediums between jinn (devils) and their customers in order to obtain information about the future. They also earned money by casting spells. They would cast a spell on a client so a devil would protect him from evil devils, and they cast spells against the enemies of their clients. Kuhhan were famous for their rhymed prose.[18] Their poetry and rhymes were hard to imitate and considered miraculous.[19] The Jinn and the Arabic Star religions went hand in hand.

Abd al-Muttalib was most famous for digging up the water well of Zamzam. That well did not exist before Abd al-Muttalib

[16] Daniel Amari, *Dawn of Islam*, 73.
[17] In the Quran, Surah 18:50 states that Satan was one of the jinn. Furthermore, Satan was described as the father of jinn. Cf. Rafat Amari, *Islam in Light of History*, 452.
[18] Rafat Amari, *Islam in Light of History*, 430.
[19] Rafat Amari, *Islam in Light of History*, 489.

dug it. The Zamzam well, a rare source of water, changed the life of Mecca. As a man very dedicated to the Jinn religion, Abd al-Muttalib sought to follow the occultic ritual concerning digging up a new well. Therefore, he dedicated the well to the jinn idols called Isaf and Na'ilah.[20] He placed two statues for them there. But the ritual required more. It required a human sacrifice. So Abd al-Muttalib took his son Abdallah to present him as a human sacrifice.[21] Abd al-Muttalib consulted with a priestess of Jinn who determined that he could sacrifice camels instead.

Abd al-Muttalib sought to marry his son Abdallah to a priestess of Jinn.[22] He met several priestesses of Jinn including one called Raqiyya bint Nofel. But he chose Amina bint Wahab.[23] There is no doubt that he selected Amina because her Aunt was Soda bint Zahra, the chief priestess of Jinn in Mecca, and thus Amina was in line to inherit her aunt's job.[24] The chief priestess position was hereditary. The child of Amina would inherit that position as well. Abdallah married Amina.

[20] Rafat Amari, *Islam in Light of History*, 388.
[21] Rafat Amari, *Islam in Light of History*, 413.
[22] Rafat Amari, *Islam in Light of History*, 408.
[23] Rafat Amari, *Islam in Light of History*, 412.
[24] Rafat Amari, *Islam in Light of History*, 412.

Amina

Amina bint Wahab, an important priestess of Jinn and the apparent heir to the chief priestess position, had several duties.[25] She earned a living from casting spells and fortune-telling as a medium between her customers and the jinn. She cast spells on the enemies of her customers. But she also cast spells on her customers upon their request. She used demons to protect her customers from the spells cast against them by other priestesses.

Priestesses of Jinn also had a duty to perform in the temple of Kaaba. Allah, one of the star deities, was worshipped at the temple of Kaaba in Mecca. But Kaaba was managed by the priestesses and priests of Jinn, called Kuhhan. The Kuhhan were famous for their rhymed prose. Clearly, they had to study and train. To become a prophet of Jinn, one had to be able to read and to acquire knowledge and teaching. Therefore, it is likely that Amina had to acquire and master multiple skills as she was being groomed for the position of high priestess of Mecca.

Then Amina was introduced (probably by her aunt, the chief priestess) to Abdallah, the son of Abd al-Muttalib, the man who dug the well of Zamzam in Mecca. Abd al-Muttalib chose Amina from among multiple priestesses.[26] She was married to

---

[25] Rafat Amari, *Islam in Light of History*, 412.
[26] Rafat Amari, *Islam in Light of History*, 412.

Abdallah, who died shortly after their marriage but not before she became pregnant with a child in the year of the elephant, 570 A.D.[27] We are told the child's name was Mohammed. Unless she married again, this child would be the future chief priest of Jinn or a prophet of Jinn.

Therefore, she raised him up as the one who would inherit her position. This meant he would be taught the priesthood art of rhymed prose and a rhythmic poetry. He would be taught the black art of casting spells and communicating with jinns (devils) as mediums do. But more importantly, he would be taught how to read. In Amina's worldview, Mohammed needed to be protected. Therefore, as a priestess, she cast spells on Mohammed at a young age, and from then on Mohammed exhibited occultic phenomena. Some claimed that he suffered from epilepsy, but the symptoms only came to him after the spells were cast on him.

Amina did not live long. She supposedly died in the year 577 A.D. We are not told the cause of her death, but we are told that her father-in-law Abd al-Muttalib assumed custody of Mohammed for a short time before he, too, died. Mohammed's uncle Abu-Talib then took custody of Mohammed. Abu-Talib was the father of Ali, and Mohammed and Ali were raised together. Like his father, Abd al-Muttalib, Abu-Talib was also very dedicated to the religious system of Mecca. One significant thing we are told about Mohammed is that Abu-Talib praised

[27] All dates based on Islamic traditions are mostly speculative.

Mohammed for his ability to cast spells.[28] This is a clear indication that the family of Mohammed successfully raised him to master the duties and skills of a priest of Jinn.

[28] Rafat Amari, *Islam in Light of History*, 490.

Waraqa ibn Nofel

Waraqa was, first and foremost, a priest of Jinn. His sister, Raqiyya bint Nofel, was a priestess of Jinn as well. She was the one Abd al-Muttalib had considered as a wife for his son Abdallah before opting instead for Amina. Waraqa came from a family very devoted to the religion of Jinn. He lived in Mecca. Once he met with three of his relatives and decided to make a local group in Mecca.[29] Zayd ibn Amru ibn Nufayl was the leader and the main founder. Waraqa was the second in command. Their group was actually a sensual, syncretistic[30], occultic religious cult. It was unknown outside of Mecca.[31]

Although members of their cult came from various religions, the common denominators of their religious beliefs were polytheism, paganism, and occultism.[32] Furthermore, participation in the Jinn religion was foundational to them. They used to practice occultic retreats in the caves of Harraa.

In addition to the Jinn religion, they shared a fascination with Sabianism, a syncretistic pagan religion influenced by Zoroastrianism. They sought religious knowledge by contacting Sabians. Sabians consisted of two groups: Mandaean Sabians

[29] Rafat Amari, *Islam in Light of History*, 410.
[30] Mixing of practices and traditions from multiple religions and cults.
[31] Rafat Amari, *Islam in Light of History*, 411.
[32] Rafat Amari, *Islam in Light of History*, 411.

and Harranian Sabians. Mandaeans lived in Mesopotamia from the 2nd century A.D. They were polytheists who worshipped personalities of light. They classified their gods into first life, second life, etc. First life created second life, and so on and so forth.[33] They lived in and around the city of Musel in Mesopotamia.[34] On the other hand, Harranian Sabians worshipped the moon, Sin, as their main deity. They worshipped other deities as well.[35]

The following are some of the Sabians' practices. They prayed 5 times per day.[36] They practiced particular movements in prayers similar to those common in Islamic practice.[37] They practiced Ablution, which is ceremonial washing, before each prayer.[38] They fasted Ramadan.[39]

Waraqa used to accompany Zayd in his travels to Northern Iraq and to Harran to learn from the Mandaeans and the Harranians.[40] They adopted many of their practices to the extent they were referred to as Sabians.[41] Because of them, the practices of Sabianism had great influence on Mecca.[42]

---

[33] Rafat Amari, *Islam in Light of History*, 434.
[34] Rafat Amari, *Islam in Light of History*, 11.
[35] Rafat Amari, *Islam in Light of History*, 434.
[36] Rafat Amari, *Islam in Light of History*, 435.
[37] Rafat Amari, *Islam in Light of History*, 435.
[38] Rafat Amari, *Islam in Light of History*, 435.
[39] Rafat Amari, *Islam in Light of History*, 435.
[40] Rafat Amari, *Islam in Light of History*, 434.
[41] Rafat Amari, *Islam in Light of History*, 435.
[42] Rafat Amari, *Islam in Light of History*, 276.

Ahnaf, as a new group, they needed to promote their cult. Therefore, their first leader, Zayd, a devotee to Sabianism who rejected Christianity and Judaism,[43] was the first to claim that Mecca and its pagan practices were tied to Abraham.[44] This was a tactic utilized by almost all pagan cults in the Middle East to gain credibility.[45]

The second strategy was to utilize sexual immorality as inducements for people to join their group.[46] Their immoral practices were documented in their poems. For example, Waraqa ibn Nofel boasted of raping a girl in her home.[47] Because of these practices, they became known as the Ahnaf (plural of hanif). In their time, the term hanif (plural Ahnaf) was a title that had a negative connotation indicating loose sexual immorality.[48] It seemed that their strategy worked on some youths. Indeed, Mohammed became a member of this group during his youth.[49] He even joined them in their retreats to the caves of Harraa.[50] Later, Mohammed would be called a Sabian by Quraysh based on his teachings.[51]

Zayd died in the late 6th century A.D., and Waraqa became the de facto leader of Ahnaf. In addition to his commitment to

---

43 Rafat Amari, *Islam in Light of History*, 12.
44 Rafat Amari, *Islam in Light of History*, 12.
45 Rafat Amari, *Star Akbar: The History of Allah, vol. 1*, 15-17.
46 Rafat Amari, *Islam in Light of History*, 411.
47 Rafat Amari, *Islam in Light of History*, 412.
48 Rafat Amari, *Islam in Light of History*, 412.
49 Rafat Amari, *Islam in Light of History*, 411.
50 Rafat Amari, *Islam in Light of History*, 11.
51 Rafat Amari, *Islam in Light of History*, 435.

the religion of Jinn, Waraqa was interested in and practiced other religions such as Sabianism and Judaism at different times in his life, but eventually became an Ebionite.[52]

Little is known about the Ebionites. They were a cult that arose most likely in the 2nd-century A.D. (at the earliest). Ebionite doctrine centered on the denial of the deity of Christ and the Trinity and the necessity of keeping the Jewish laws and regulations.

Waraqa also had great interest in Gnosticism. Gnosticism was a pagan religious-philosophical system that began during the 2nd century A.D. The core of Gnosticism is Platonism[53] infused with Persian ideas and wrapped in a strong emphasis on dualism. In a way, it is a later reinterpretation of Platonism utilizing Christian terminology. The Gnostics selectively co-opted some Christian and Jewish names and expressions in their system. Gnosticism's main contribution to Arabia is the denial of the crucifixion of Christ.

Waraqa's interest in various cults and religions led to a syncretistic mixture of Gnostic/Ebionite doctrines about Jesus, such as the denial of the following Christian doctrines: the deity of Christ, the Trinity, and the crucifixion of Christ.[54] All of this

---

[52] Rafat Amari, *Islam in Light of History*, 12, 410.

[53] Platonism a philosophy based on Plato's ideas, the notion that earthly things are imperfect copies of things that exist in their perfect form in the non-earthly realm.

[54] Dr. Rafat Amari points out that Waraqa was not the only source of Gnosticism and pagan and Christian heresies. Umayya bin abi al-Salt was

was combined with Sabian rituals and Jinn occultism.[55] One could say that Waraqa and his Ahnaf cult were all about new religions and sexual hedonism.

also an important source through his poems. Umayya was also a member of Ahnaf, a fact that could explain the connection. For full treatment of this subject, cf. *Star Akbar: The History of Allah, vol. 1*, 205.

[55] Rafat Amari, *Islam in Light of History*, 410.

Khadija

Her full name was Khadija bint Khuwaylid. She came from a family that was immersed in the Jinn religion. She was also dedicated to that religion, for it made her rich. Despite the fact that she came from a poor family, Khadija was very wealthy. If somebody was rich in Mecca, it was because he or she was either a prophet of Jinn or owned trading caravans. Khadija owned trading caravans. Here is her story.

Khadija was married to Nabash ibn Zarara.[56] This was either her first or second marriage.[57] Nabash was a prophet of Jinn, which explains Khadija's initial source of wealth. His status also gave her some prestige in Mecca. She invested her wealth in running caravans.[58]

Khadija wanted to expand her wealth. But more importantly, she wanted to expand her influence. Before Islam, women could be leaders of tribes, cities, and nations. After Nabash died, Khadija had the wealth but lost the prestige and the power she enjoyed as the wife of a prophet of Jinn. This did not stop Khadija, however. She discovered that one of her workers, Mohammed, was the only son of the famous Amina, the heir of

---

[56] Rafat Amari, *Islam in Light of History*, 409.
[57] It is possible that Khadija had a previous marriage.
[58] Rafat Amari, *Islam in Light of History*, 409.

the Jinn chief priestess position. More importantly, he had all the qualifications one needed to be a prophet of Jinn, a replacement for Nabash. According to Islamic tradition, Mohammed was about 20 years younger than Khadija. Being the strong woman she was, however, Khadija did not hesitate and proposed marriage to him.[59]

Mohammed continued to be a member of the Ahnaf and to go on retreats to the caves of Harraa. Ever since his mother, Amina, cast spells on him, Mohammed was subject to experiencing occultic symptoms. These symptoms took a turn for the worse in Harraa. In particular, he had a negative experience where a spiritual entity appeared to him and tried to choke him into submission. The name that Mohammed gave to that spirit was "death." Khadija saw this as the opportunity she was seeking. From her worldview, this was a successful contact with the world of jinn at the highest level. Immediately she told Mohammed that he was a prophet.[60]

Mohammed himself, however, was not convinced. He insisted that he was ill and that a devil was in him. The symptoms became worse, and Mohammed even attempted to commit suicide. Khadija was not able to help him. Mohammed would not submit to the spirit and embrace his wife's calling as a prophet. Finally, Khadija sought the help of her cousin, an

[59] Rafat Amari, *Islam in Light of History*, 409.
[60] Rafat Amari, *Islam in Light of History*, 490.

experienced priest of Jinn, to convince Mohammed that he was a prophet. Her cousin's name was Waraqa ibn Nofel.[61]

By now Waraqa was old and blind and was looking for a leader he could train to lead the Ahnaf.[62] Waraqa became Mohammed's mentor and began to teach him and to prepare him to take over the Ahnaf. He transmitted to him the various teachings he learned about Jinn religion, Sabianism, Gnosticism, and Ebionism.

In the meantime, Khadija did not wait for Mohammed to be convinced. She began to proclaim him a prophet to other people. That continued for several years. Although she had limited influence, the followers of Nabash, her previous husband, became followers of Mohammed on account of her. They numbered about 20. The most important of the followers, and the most loyal, was named Abu Bakr.

The occultic episodes did not stop but continued and became worse to the extent that the dark spirit was choking Mohammed and almost killing him. Mohammed finally submitted to the dark spirit, however, and learned to accept that he was a prophet per Khadija's wishes.[63] A prophet of Jinn had to be able to provide new teaching and new verses in a framework of rhymed prose. Mohammed had no problems doing

[61] Rafat Amari, *Islam in Light of History*, 409.
[62] Rafat Amari, *Islam in Light of History*, 409.
[63] Islamic tradition places the time for Mohammed's public announcement as a prophet around 610 A.D. The exact dates, however, are all speculative.

so, for Waraqa taught him the verses of the Quran[64] for this period. Waraqa was the true source. Mohammed needed all the support he could get. Dr. Rafat Amari states, "Mohammed continued to consult the Kuhhan and the Jinn religion of Arabia even after he claimed to be a prophet."[65]

But everything did not go so well after Waraqa died.[66] The verses of the Quran stopped[67] coming to Mohammed for an obvious reason: Waraqa was the source. Mohammed repeatedly wanted to commit suicide by throwing himself from a mountain cliff. There is disagreement on how long this period lasted – estimate range somewhere between 40 days and three years.[68]

Khadija's plan did not achieve the desired results. She needed to dominate Mecca. But the people of Quraysh were not convinced by Mohammed's claims. The only followers of Mohammed in this period were the followers of Nabash. Worse

[64] At this point, and during the life of Mohammed, the Quran was not written down.
[65] Rafat Amari, *Islam in Light of History*, 485.
[66] It is not clear when Waraqa died. Books of Islamic tradition contradict each other on this point. But the most historically compelling narration suggests that he died sometime after Mohammed publicly claimed to be a prophet, yet before the migration to Yathrib. The statement that the Quran stopped coming to Mohammed after the death of Waraqa implies that Waraqa was alive during Mohammed's Da'wa (religious calling) and Mohammed was dependent on him for the verses of the Quran. Waraqa was his true mentor.
[67] The Arabic verb fatara (فتر) literally means cooled down. It could mean that they stopped. It also could suggest that the verses of the Quran came to Mohammed less frequently and not with the same quality as the ones by Waraqa.
[68] Rafat Amari, *Islam in Light of History*, 412.

than this, after Waraqa's death, no compelling new teaching came to Mohammed to continue the religious strategy of peaceful proselytization. Thus, a new strategy was needed to accomplish Khadija's goal.

The new strategy involved switching from peaceful proselytization to piracy and violence. So Mohammed gathered about 80 followers, most of them outlaws and criminals who attacked trade caravans, and they ventured out on a new campaign not to proselytize but to pillage. They robbed, raped, and murdered people.[69] Mohammed received a cut of all the spoils. Al-Bukhari[70] described them using the Arabic term "gang."[71]

Mohammed was more successful with piracy than with religious proselytization. But that was not enough for Khadija, who began sending Mohammed out to visit Arabian tribes and offer them a deal for joining Mohammed.[72]

While Mohammed was married to Khadija, he was not able to take additional wives or own any concubines. This had nothing to do with Mohamamed's moral or religious convictions or those of Khadija. It had everything to do with Khadija's control over him. In a way, this was not the story of Mohammed as much as it was the story of Khadija. But the day came when

[69] Rafat Amari, *Islam in Light of History*, 449.
[70] The most authoritative compiler of Hadith.
[71] Rafat Amari, *Islam in Light of History*, 449.
[72] Rafat Amari, *Islam in Light of History*, 450.

Khadija died.[73] Her vision of global domination of Mecca and Arabia was not achieved. But she managed to accomplish one thing; she converted Mohammed into a believer in her vision of the domination of Arabia.

Mohammed continued the strategy with the support-system his late wife built. He visited many Arabian tribes and made them an offer. For their part, they were to join him, accept him as a prophet, venerate Allah as the higher deity above Allah's wife and daughters, and war against other tribes. In return, they would get the belongings of other tribes. They would make the other tribes' women and daughters concubines and take their children as slaves.[74] Arabian tribes strongly rejected his offer. They told Mohammed that he was dishonorable even to suggest that they commit such crimes against their brethren tribes.[75] Islamic tradition states that after one of the rejections, Mohammed was very discouraged, but the jinn came to encourage him.[76] Dr. Rafat Amari adds:

> The Jinn-devils immediately began authoring a chapter in the Quran equal in language to the rest of the Quran, attacking the Sonship of Christ and boasting to be righteous.[77]

[73] Some Islamic traditions, such as Ibn Hisham, Al-Tabari, and Al-Halabiyya, place the death of Khadija at about 619 A.D., about three years before the migration to Yathrib, but that is disputed.
[74] Rafat Amari, *Islam in Light of History*, 451.
[75] Rafat Amari, *Islam in Light of History*, 451.
[76] Rafat Amari, *Islam in Light of History*, 451.
[77] Rafat Amari, *Islam in Light of History*, 452.

Aws & Khazraj

Aws and Khazraj were two savage tribes who lived near the city of Yathrib. The city was later named al-Medina. Yathrib was a far more ancient city than Mecca by more than a millennium. Mecca was built in the 4th century A.D. Dr. Rafat Amari describes these two tribes as follows:

> Their members were known for their lives of frivolity and violence. They were known for being lazy, not willing to work, and living from freeloading off others.[78]

Furthermore, they were pagan tribes. They had their own rituals and practiced them devoutly. They were very much attached to the religion of Jinn. They had strong devotion to the idols of Isaf and Na'ila and all the pagan rituals associated with these idols.

Among the inhabitants of the city were several Jewish tribes. Two of them were called Bani Quraytha and Bani al-Nathir. Dr. Rafat Amari states, "they were known to cultivate the land and plant trees—mainly dates. They built commerce between Syria and Arabia."[79] Aws and Khazraj were dependent

---

[78] Rafat Amari, *Islam in Light of History*, 455.
[79] Rafat Amari, *Islam in Light of History*, 455.

on the Jewish tribes and often received much help from them. That was the situation in the city of Yathrib at that time.

The status quo in Yathrib changed when Mohammed approached the Aws and Khazraj with his offer. He enticed them with the following ploy: why settle for *some* help from the Jewish tribes when they, Aws and Khazraj, could take it all—including their women? In the Islamic traditions, there is a long list of the names of Arabian tribes that rejected Mohammed's offer. Aws and Khazraj, however, accepted it, considering it a great opportunity.

They entered into negotiations with Mohammed. Aws and Khazraj were concerned about religious rituals they observed.[80] There were differences between Mohammed's practices and their practices. For example, Aws and Khazraj prayed towards Mecca instead of towards Jerusalem.[81] To Mohammed, Mecca at this point was not that important, until the leaders of Aws and Khazraj imposed it on him.[82] They worshipped on Friday.

[80] Rafat Amari, *Islam in Light of History*, 427.
[81] Rafat Amari, *Islam in Light of History*, 437.
[82] Rafat Amari, *Islam in Light of History*, 473. It is important to keep in mind that Mecca was occupied later, possibly only few years before Mohammed's sudden death. This was later followed by the short rule of Abu Bakr and then Umar. When Uthman and the Umayyads came to power, they had different priorities from Mecca. In the second half of the 7th century A.D., Damascus eventually replaced Yathrib as the political capital of the Islamic state. Furthermore, Mecca's role as the sacred capital of Islam was under strong attack from the Umayyads until they controlled it. All of this history must be taken into consideration when examining the Qibla's history. It is more complicated than the switch from Jerusalem to Mecca, and it possibly involved other destinations such as Tabuk and others.

Mohammed made it the Islamic day.[83] They had a pagan ritual that involved the mountains Safa and Marwa.[84] Some Muslims objected to and refused to participate in it. But behold a verse of Quran came to Mohammed that legislated the ritual for Muslims.[85] During the great Hajj, pilgrimage to holy places, Aws and Khazraj had an additional final stop at the Kaaba in Mecca to worship Isaf and Na'ila. Mohammed complied with them and instituted this additional stop in the great Hajj to this day.[86]

What did Mohammed demand in return? One would expect some important religious rituals of his own. But that was not the case. Instead, he demanded absolute and perfect obedience from the two tribes in all circumstances and a guarantee that he would personally receive one-fifth of all the spoils and all the women from their massacre of the various tribes.[87]

After the deal was made, Mohammed emigrated to al-Medina (Yathrib).[88] Islamic traditions state it was around 622 A.D.[89] One might wonder how some humans could slaughter and rape an entire Jewish tribe. Dr. Amari sheds light on this:

[83] Rafat Amari, *Islam in Light of History*, 438.
[84] Rafat Amari, *Islam in Light of History*, 474.
[85] Rafat Amari, *Islam in Light of History*, 423.
[86] Rafat Amari, *Islam in Light of History*, 387.
[87] Rafat Amari, *Islam in Light of History*, 462.
[88] Rafat Amari, *Islam in Light of History*, 455.
[89] As with all dates from Islamic traditions, one must exercise caution.

> Mohammed was hatching a plan to expel and kill them [the Jewish tribes] while defiling their women and plundering their possessions. Thus, he sought to reduce them to the level of monkeys and pigs to justify killing them in the same manner as unclean animals.[90]

This is when the verses of the Quran that talk about Jewish tribes transforming into pigs and monkeys appeared. The Quran also stated that the Jews were infidels and the worst of all creatures. After arriving in al-Medina (Yathrib), Mohammed besieged the settlements of Bani al-Nathir. Let Dr. Amari take up the story:

> [Mohammed] took their houses and prohibited food from reaching them. The lack of food made them yield to him. So Mohammed took their houses, furniture, and fields and all their gold, money, and weapons. Once deported from the city the Jewish tribe of Bani Nathir went to Syria. Later, Mohammed besieged the second Jewish tribe, Bani Quraytha and prohibited food and water from reaching them… All males over ten years of age were killed, and the males under ten became slaves. The houses, and the females of the tribe, were derived and given to Mohammed's followers… With the money obtained from selling the older women and the children as slaves, he built an army and equipped them with body armor and shields. Now he was prepared to wage war against other Arabian cities and to subdue them.[91]

---

[90] Rafat Amari, *Quran & History*, 475.
[91] Rafat Amari, *Islam in Light of History*, 456.

There was a place called Thaniat al-Wadaa located in the suburbs of Yathrib. The Islamic traditions state that it was the place where they gathered the Jewish women and girls and raped them.[92]

With the help of these two tribes Aws and Khazraj, Mohammed grew in power and his army in number. Now he controlled a city from which he could dominate Arabia. Kuhhan, priests of Jinn, backed Mohammed's claim to prophecy and promoted Islam.[93] In fact, after Mohammed emigrated to Medina, many kuhhan fought alongside him.[94] Kuhhan used their poems to praise Mohammed. Hassan ibn Thabet, a poet, confessed that a devil inspired his poetry.[95]

There Mohammed also met Selman al-Farsi, a Zoroastrian priest of advanced rank. Zoroastrianism is a Persian religion that practices polytheism while declaring monotheism. Some have labeled it henotheism because in doctrine extols belief in one God while in practice multiple deities are honored. The system had evolved from its ancient polytheistic roots to a more recent monotheistic claim. This evolution came about from the influence of Judaism. Despite its strong claims of monotheism, such a religion can never escape its roots. There are still multiple deities in Zoroastrianism. For example, there are the main dualistic deities, Ahura-Mazda, representing good, and

---

[92] Rafat Amari, *Islam in Light of History*, 478.
[93] Rafat Amari, *Islam in Light of History*, 487.
[94] Rafat Amari, *Islam in Light of History*, 488.
[95] Rafat Amari, *Islam in Light of History*, 489.

Ahriman, representing evil. Zoroastrians venerated the star Tistrya (Tishtrya) as the lord of the stars.[96]

Mohammed found a new source of teaching. So he made Selman al-Farsi his counselor and rewarded him with gold. Behold the verses of Quran started to flow again richly with new teachings. But this time, they were Zoroastrian teachings.[97] Islam was no longer a religious cult for pirates but a seed of nation-state.

[96] Rafat Amari, *Islam in Light of History*, 446.
[97] Rafat Amari, *Quran & History*, 28.

Abu Sufyan

Abu Sufyan ibn Harb was from the tribe of Abd-Shams of Quraysh. Abd-Shams means the slave of the sun. They worshipped mainly Allat (the sun). They also worshipped her daughters such as al-Uzza. Each tribe in Arabia had their own main deities, and Quraysh was no exception. Abu Sufyan was described as one of the nobles of Quraysh and considered to be its leader and an honorable man. He was a trader by profession. He took caravans to the Byzantine empire for trade.

Abu Sufyan, along with the rest of Quraysh, first heard about Mohammed's claim of prophecy from Khadija. She insisted that Mohammed was a prophet. Abu Sufyan figured out Khadija and saw her designs for what they were—a play for power. Her previous husband was Nabash, the prophet of Jinn. She had the wealth, but what was she after? And why had Mohammed not come out and declared himself to be a prophet. Abu Sufyan and the rest of Quraysh were skeptical. For several years, Khadija had been calling on Quraysh to accept Mohammed as a prophet. But only a few accepted him, the followers of Nabash.

Finally, when Mohammed came out and declared he was a prophet, there was an expectation that he would present new teaching. He did not. To Abu Sufyan, he was simply parroting rhymed prose of the old man Waraqa, the cousin of Khadija. Clearly, there was a conspiracy between Khadija and her cousin. There was nothing new, only what they had already heard from Waraqa, from the Sabians, and from his cousin Umayya ibn Abi al-Salt.

What was more troubling for Abu-Sufyan was the fact that Mohammed repackaged old claims about Allah and tried to impose them on Quraysh. Namely, during Mohammed's time, Allah was an exclusive title and an identifying name of a pagan deity known as the Star. It is also known by other names all over Arabia. It is basically the planet Venus. As several others before him, Mohammed tried to elevate Allah above his wife Allat (the Sun) and his daughters. Mohammed insisted that Allah was greater than Allat and his daughters, Uzza and Manat. Quraysh had heard this before from a prophet of the city of Yamama called Maslama ibn Habib.[98] He wanted to elevate al-Rahman (Venus) as well. They all used the slogan, *la ilah illa Allah* (There is no god but Allah). Even the priestess and priests of Jinn used that slogan.

Traditionally, Quraysh elevated the female deities of Allat and al-Uzza. Mohammed was trying to shake up the order of the deities and elevate the male deity instead.[99] Abu Sufyan did not trust Khadija and her cousin Waraqa, but he tried to get Mohammed's uncle Abu Lahab involved and also Amru ibn

[98] For a full treatment of the influence of Maslama on Mohammed, cf. *Star Akbar: The History of Allah, vol. 1*, 55.
[99] Rafat Amari, *Islam in Light of History*, 273-279. Rafat Amari, *Star Akbar: The History of Allah, vol. 1*, 375.

Hisham[100] to help talk some sense into Mohammed. Khadija and Waraqa, however, were formidable. Clearly, some tension was afoot. Mohammed was annoying everyone, and Khadija was frustrated with the lack of results. The people of Quraysh were simply not convinced.

There were times when Mohammed was able to get along with Quraysh. For example, the time Mohammed told Quraysh that he still honored Allat, Uzza, and Manat. He claimed that they were like angels in the sky. For Quraysh, speaking well about their deities was a good beginning of cordial relationships, which led to Mohammed, Quraysh, and the rest of Muslims praying together to all the members of the Arabian star family religion: Allah, Allat, Uzza, and Manat. Of course, Quraysh did not accept the rest of the system that Allah was the higher deity, and that all the female deities of Quraysh were not females but only angels that can receive prayers and intercede with Allah's permission.[101]

For Abu Sufyan, as long as the differences were theological, the trade was intact, and lives were not in danger, Mohammed could be tolerated. Maybe his uncle and some folks from his tribe could help him see the game that Khadija and Waraqa were playing. Then again, Khadija and Waraqa were both old and would not live forever.

---

[100] Muslim narrators called him Abu Jahl (the father of ignorance). Nevertheless, he was one of the nobles of Quraysh.
[101] Rafat Amari, *Islam in Light of History*, 280-281. Rafat Amari, *Star Akbar: The History of Allah, vol.1*, 375.

Clearly, Abu Sufyan's assessment was wrong. Mohammed and Khadija began practicing piracy and attacking the caravans of Quraysh. They were joined by outlaws and a number of folks from Mecca. To Abu Sufyan and the rest of Quraysh, this was a confirmation that this had nothing to do with religion. It was all a power play by Khadija and Mohammed, who fully embraced it. Abu-Sufyan's responded by getting extra security for the caravans. Quraysh thought this would limit Mohammed greatly, especially after Khadija died.

But Abu-Sufyan and Quraysh thought wrong again. The savage tribes, Aws and Khazraj, had joined Mohammed. They attacked Medina and slaughtered all males 10 years and older. They had no mercy on older men and women. They plundered, raped, and enslaved. More alarmingly, some young men of Mecca were lured by Mohammed and joined him.

Mohammed went after the caravans, especially those that came from Syria. While Abu Sufyan was leading a trade caravan from Syria, reports came to him about Mohammed sending his followers to attack the caravans.[102] Abu Sufyan did two things. First, he took another route. Second, he asked for help from Quraysh in Mecca. When the nobles of Mecca heard of this, they went out to defend their trade and their people who were leading the caravan. They knew that if Mohammed found the caravan, he would slaughter the whole party. The caravan reached Mecca safely, so the original goal of Mohammed failed. When the

[102] Tarikh al-Tabari, part 2, 22.

nobles met with Mohammed, however, Mohammed took revenge. Let Dr. Amari pick up the story:

> When Mohammed saw that many of the people of Mecca were the fathers of his followers, he intentionally ordered his Muslim followers to war with and fight their own fathers. Mohammed knew the fathers would not kill their sons, even though they (the sons) joined Mohammed and sabotaged the law and the security of the city. Mohammed knew this, and he saw that he would gain an advantage in battle when he selected sons to fight their own fathers. As a result, many fathers were killed by their own Muslim sons during the battle.[103]

This happened during the fasting of Ramadan that Mohammed ordered, which was supposed to be a time of peace, reflection, and spirituality. Amru ibn Hisham was killed.[104] Abu Sufyan and Quraysh underestimated the danger and cruelty of Mohammed. They also underestimated the expansionist ideology of this new state. This state could not produce economically to sustain its people. It needed a constant supply of spoils from conquering new cities. As it expanded, it transformed new converts to Islam into soldiers. This required more cities to plunder.

Therefore, several years later when Mohammed attacked Mecca, it was with a significantly larger army. And Quraysh lost

[103] Rafat Amari, *Islam in Light of History*, 481.

[104] Muslim narrators called this attack the Battle of Badr. They claimed that the angels helped Mohammed against the infidels of Quraysh.

the battle.[105] Abu Sufyan acted quickly. He wanted to save the people of Mecca from being slaughtered. There was one path for them. He, along with many of his tribe, the Umayyads, pretended to embrace Islam. He was literally forced to become a Muslim. [106] Furthermore, he negotiated a surrender with Mohammed so that all those who sought protection under the roof of Abu Sufyan would be safe.[107] Mohammed's assurances to Abu Sufyan, however, did not prevent the group rape of the women of Mecca, as was the pattern of each plunder.

Abu Sufyan was now forced to join the army of Mohammed and attack other tribes and nations. The former leader of Quraysh and his tribe, Abu Sufyan's children, nephews, and his relatives watched how he and subsequently their tribe was shamed as this narration illustrates:

[105] Islamic traditions place the conquering of Mecca around 630 A.D.
[106] Sahih al-Bukhari, Kitab al-Jihad wa al-Siyar, Bab Du'a al-Nabi ila al-Islam wa al-Nubuwwa, 2941.
[107] Sahih Muslim, Kitab al-Jihad wa al-Siyar, Bab Fath Mecca, 4622.

Abu Bakr, may Allah be pleased with him, received a report about something that Abu Sufyan Sakhr ibn Harb did. So Abu Bakr brought Abu Sufyan and began to yell at him, while Abu Sufyan was begging him and being subservient to him, and Abu Qahhafa came and heard the yelling of Abu Bakr, he said to his commander, "Who my son is yelling at?" The commander replied, "At Abu Sufyan." So he approached Abu Bakr and said to him, "On Abu Sufyan you dare to raise your voice, O Atiq-Allah? Yesterday, Abu Sufyan was the master of Quraish in Jahiliyyah. You have trespassed your limits and exceeded your magnitude." Abu Bakr smiled and those with him from Muslim immigrants and supporters, and said to him, "Father, in Islam, Allah raised some and humiliated the others."[108]

[108] Masudi, *Muruj al-Thahab*, part 2, 236.

THE SPREAD OF ISLAM

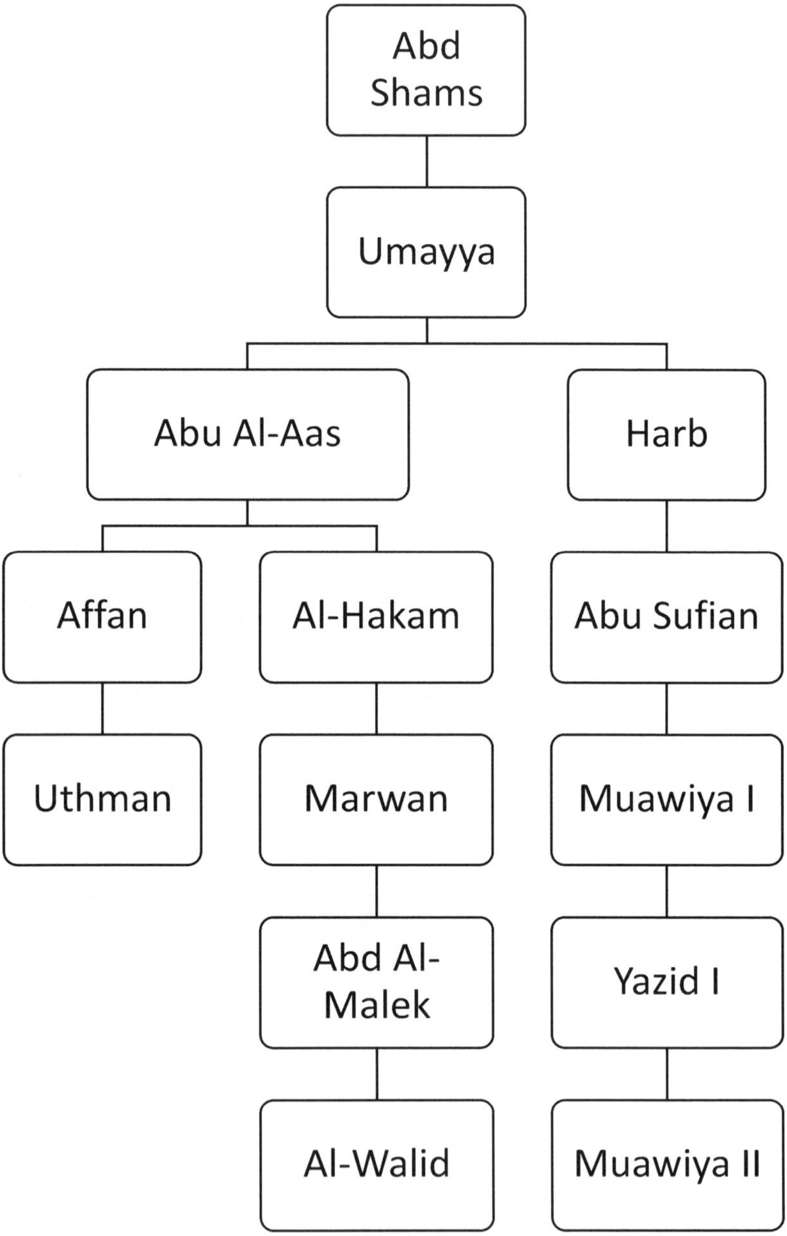
Abd Shams
Umayya
Abu Al-Aas
Harb
Affan
Al-Hakam
Abu Sufian
Uthman
Marwan
Muawiya I
Abd Al-Malek
Yazid I
Al-Walid
Muawiya II

Introduction to the Spread of Islam

There are two important and interconnected observations about the spread of Islam. First, the struggle for who will be the next caliph (religious and political ruler) dominated the history of Islam even before the death of Mohammed. Second, the evolution of the Quran was a direct consequence of that struggle.

Abu Bakr	First companion of Mohammed and second in command. First caliph after the death of Mohammed.
Hafsa	One of the wives of Mohammed. The daughter of Umar ibn al-Khattab, the second caliph.
Ibn Masud	One of the most important men whom Mohammed assigned the task of memorizing the Quran for safekeeping.
Marwan	An important cousin of Uthman ibn Affan, the third caliph. From the Umayyad Dynasty.
Al-Hajjaj	Powerful military ruler working for Umayyad Dynasty.

Abu Bakr

He was known by the title Atiq. He was a loyal disciple of Mohammad's first wife, Khadija, and her previous husband, Nabash. After Nabash died, Abu Bakr remained loyal to Khadija. After all, the wife of the prophet of Jinn was also considered a prophetess of Jinn. Khadija was a rich and powerful woman. Abu Bakr was loyal and obedient to her and later became loyal and obedient to Mohammed.[109] He became the most important disciple of Mohammed. From his perspective, he sacrificed so much for Mohammed and Khadija that one could say he sold his soul to them.

Abu Bakr's involvement with Mohammed began when Khadija asked him to bring Mohammed to Waraqa. For at least three years, Mohammed was not convinced that he was a prophet. He said that he was ill and that a demon was in him. Yet Khadija asked Abu Bakr to proselytize on behalf of Mohammed during this period. When proselytizing did not bear fruit, he began to purchase slaves and prisoners on the condition that they first embrace Islam. For the record, Mohammed was not against slavery. In Mohammed's lifetime, especially after his migration to Medina, he enslaved people including children and

[109] Rafat Amari, *Quran & History*, 477.

sold slaves, owned slaves, and had great contempt towards African slaves.[110]

Abu Bakr always accompanied Khadija and Mohammed, and when Khadija died he was loyal to Mohammed as he had been loyal to Nabash before him. He knew that the whole campaign was for money and power. And he realized that he had a role to play and a share of the spoils to grab.

One of Mohammed's more significant prophetic claims was that he took a journey to the Jewish temple[111] in Jerusalem and returned the same night.[112] Of course, the Jewish temple had been destroyed by the Roman general Titus in 70 A.D. Nevertheless, Mohammed insisted that he actually saw the temple, prayed inside it, and met the Christian and Jewish "prophets." Mohammed claimed that he was more significant than they, for he led them in prayer. Concerning the great distance traveled in one night, Mohammed claimed that he rode a winged mammal called al-Buraq.[113] Quraysh challenged these claims: if Mohammed had truly traveled from Mecca all the way to Jerusalem and back in one night and entered the temple, then he would have no problem describing the temple. Under this

---

[110] Asqalani, *Fath al-Bari*, part 13, 122 (commenting on Sahih al-Bukhari 7142).
[111] What Mohammed used is the term Beit al-Maqdes, a known term in Arabia referring to the Jewish Temple, which is equivalent to Beit haMiqdash.
[112] This incident is called al-Isra'.
[113] Rafat Amari, *Quran & History*, 373-377. The western wall is called by Muslims al-Buraq till today. Some Islamic traditions claim it was a winged flying donkey or horse.

challenge, Mohammed collapsed. He had no answers, and his countenance betrayed deep guilt mixed with intense panic.[114] Abu Bakr had seen previous blunders of Mohammed, but never like this. This was about to spell the end of Mohammed and his prophetic claims.

Abu Bakr needed to act quickly, and he did. In front of everybody, he asked Mohammed to describe the Jewish temple, for he claimed that he himself had visited the temple and had seen it. He offered to verify to other people, including Muslim converts, that Mohammed was a true prophet. Of course, Abu Bakr knew he was lying, but he needed to save Mohammed. Mohammed proceeded to describe the temple, its door, its windows, and other details. Abu Bakr confirmed each description with the words, "You have spoken the truth. Truly you are the apostle of Allah." At the end, on account of Abu Bakr's testimony on his behalf, Mohammed gave him the title al-Siddiq, the righteous one. From that day forward, he was known as Abu Bakr al-Siddiq.[115]

After his wife, Khadija, died, Mohammed experienced a major change. He had been living in fear of her, but was at last free and started owning and sleeping with concubines and getting wives. It was as if he was the most deprived man on earth. He replaced the older concubines with younger ones. Mohammed approached Abu Bakr and declared that he would

[114] Rafat Amari, *Quran & History*, 379.
[115] Rafat Amari, *Quran & History*, 380.

marry Abu Bakr's daughter Aisha. She was 6 years old,[116] and Mohammed was 54.[117] This was the place where most loyalists would have drawn the line. According to the Arabic author Jamil Suleiman, "Abu Bakr, the father of Aisha, had tried to dissuade Mohammed from his desire for his child but to no avail."[118] The actual plea he used with Mohammed can be expressed as follows, "Please do not do this to me, I am your brother." The actual answer of Mohammed was, "Yes. You are my brother in the religion of Allah and his book; but she is halal[119] for me."[120] Mohammed claimed that Allah told him that Aisha would be his wife.[121] No one had been as loyal to Mohammed as Abu Bakr, and no one had sacrificed as much. He sacrificed his own daughter.

The desires of Mohammed became more intense. Every woman Mohammed desired, he took. It did not matter how old she was, whether she was married, or whether she was a Muslima. There was no limit. Any husband or father who

[116] Both Sahih Bukhari and Sahih Muslim state that Mohammed married her at 6 and had sexual relationships with her at 9. Later Islamic historical books tried to find a way out of this. This is an indication of the authenticity of the narration and that it was not an acceptable age of marriage for Arabian tribes at that time. It is consistent with the objections of Abu Bakr and the overall pattern of Mohammed's sexual behavior.
[117] Sahih al-Bukhari, Kitab Manaqib al-Ansar, Bab Tazwij al-Nabi, 3894-3896.
[118] Jamil Sulayman, *Taalu ila Kalima Sawa'*, 131.
[119] Halal: Moral and Legal by decree of Allah.
[120] Sahih al-Bukhari, Kitab al-Nikah, Bab Tazwij al-Sighar min al-Kibar, 5081.
[121] Sahih al-Bukhari, Kitab al-Nikah, Bab al-Nathar ila al-Imraa qabl al-Tazwij, 5125.

opposed Mohammed in that regard was killed. One would wonder if women began to cover their heads and faces as protection in that context. Mohammed had an adopted son. He was known as Zayd ibn (son of) Mohammed.[122] He was adopted as a child by Mohammed and Khadija. When his biological father tried to get him back, Mohammed refused and insisted that Zayd remain with him as his son.[123] He was married to a beautiful woman called Zaynab bint Jahsh. Let Dr. Amari continue the story:

> Zayd was not in his house when Zaynab, Zayd's wife, opened the door for Mohammed. The wind lifted up her clothing before Mohammed and, as a result, Mohammed desired her and expressed this openly to her. When Zayd returned back home, his wife told him about Mohammed's desire for her. Zayd, knowing that every female whom Mohammed desired should be given to him, went to Mohammed and told him that he would leave his wife for Mohammed's sake. The next day Mohammed brought a verse from the Quran, the 37th verse of surah 33, called al-Ahzab, which claimed that Allah gave Zayd's wife to him. He also authorized Muslims to marry their daughters-in-law if their adopted sons leave their wives.[124]

This event was great insight for Abu Bakr. He realized how powerful the Quran was as a tool to control the people. Muslims were horrified at the practices of Mohammed but accepted them when he gave them a verse from the Quran. Abu Bakr and future

---

[122] Tarikh al-Tabari, part 2, 104.
[123] Rafat Amari, *Islam in Light of History*, 71.
[124] Rafat Amari, *Islam in Light of History*, 70-71.

caliphs realized that the way to exert control over Muslims was through legislation through the Quran.

Abu Bakr felt that he was owed the right to take over after Mohammed and to become the first caliph. The term caliph means a ruler who is both a successor and representative of somebody else. Abu Bakr understood the term as the caliph of Mohammed. To him, who better to fill that position than he!

Mohammed, however, still had strong feelings for his adopted son, Zayd. He appointed him as the general leader of the Islamic army. [125] When Abu Bakr protested, Mohammed declared that he loved Zayd the most.[126] To Abu Bakr, Zayd was an obstacle, for clearly Mohammed was making Zayd the second in command instead of him. But Zayd was killed, which resolved the problem.[127]

The matter, however, became worse. Mohammed decided to appoint his grandson Usama, the son of his adopted son Zayd, as the leader of the army.[128] This despite the fact that Usama was as young as 17 years of age and had no experience. [129] To Mohammed, Usama was his legacy. When Abu Bakr and Umar strongly protested, [130] Mohammed became "extremely very angry" and insisted that he loved Usama the most and asked

---

[125] Tarikh al-Tabari, part 2, 149-150.
[126] Sira al-Halabiyya, Part 3, 292.
[127] Although Zayd was supposedly killed in the battle of Mu'ta, the Islamic accounts of this battle contain many historical problems. There are no reputable accounts of how Zayd was killed.
[128] Tarikh al-Tabari, part 2, 266.
[129] Sira al-Halabiyya, Part 3, 291.
[130] Sira al-Halabiyya, Part 3, 291.

everybody to support him.[131] To Abu Bakr, this was a clear indication that Mohammed intended to pass the leadership of all Muslims to Usama. Abu Bakr had no problem with giving a role to Usama but not at the expense of his being caliph. Mohammed favored his house over Abu Bakr, and here Mohammed crossed Abu Bakr's red line. Contrary to the orders of Mohammed, Abu Bakr did not join Usama.[132]

Clearly, Mohammed had to go. So Abu Bakr asked his daughter Aisha to find an opportunity to poison Mohammed. At the same time Mohammed became suspicious of assassination attempts against him and instructed everyone not to give him anything while he was sleeping.[133] Aisha, however, managed to place some substance in his mouth while he was sleeping. When Mohammed discovered it, he was angry and threatened to have everybody present except for his uncle al-Abbas dosed with the same substance.[134] Clearly, he did not trust any of his family members except for his uncle. And clearly, they were not able to find that poison.

So how did Aisha defend herself? Initially, she claimed that she had only given him medicine, even though Mohammed had strictly instructed everyone not to do so while he was sleeping.[135] Then Aisha accused al-Abbas.[136] Then she accused

---

131 Sira al-Halabiyya, Part 3, 292.
132 Sira al-Halabiyya, part 3, 292.
133 Sahih al-Bukhari, Kitab al-Maghazi, Bab Maradh al-Nabi, 4458.
134 Sahih al-Bukhari, Kitab al-Maghazi, Bab Maradh al-Nabi, 6886. Sahih Muslim, 5761.
135 Sira al-Halabiyya, part 3, 497.
136 Tarikh al-Tabari, part 2, 273.

Ethiopian women.[137] Then she accused Asma'.[138] When it became clear that the substance was not a medicine but a slow poison, Aisha claimed that Mohammed was poisoned by a Jewish woman during the attack on Khaybar.[139] The attack on Khaybar, however, had occurred more than three years earlier.[140]

When Mohammed discovered he had been poisoned and that his companions were going to rob him of his legacy, he decided to recant and ruin it for them. He asked for a pencil and a tablet to write on.[141] He stated that he wanted to write a book for them that would prevent them from ever being deceived again.[142] Some of the Muslims wanted to give Mohammed something to write on, while others strongly objected.[143] Abu Bakr also felt that this final play by Mohammed was dangerous. But Umar, the ally of Abu Bakr intercepted. First, Umar prevented Mohammed from writing whatever he wanted to

137 Tarikh al-Tabari, part 2, 273.
138 Tarikh al-Tabari, part 2, 273.
139 Sira al-Halabiyya, part 3, 486. Sahih al-Bukhari, 5777. Sahih al-Bukhari, Kitab al-Maghazi, Bab Maradh al-Nabi, 4428.
140 It is amazing how eventually Jewish people got accused, which is the most accepted explanation today.
141 Sahih al-Bukhari, Kitab al-Maghazi, Bab Maradh al-Nabi, 4432. Sahih Muslim, Kitab al-Wasiya, Bab Tark al-Wasiya, 4233, 4234. Tarikh al-Tabari, part 2, 271.
142 Sahih al-Bukhari, Kitab al-Maghazi, Bab Maradh al-Nabi, 4432. Sahih Muslim, Kitab al-Wasiya, Bab Tark al-Wasiya, 4233, 4234. Tarikh al-Tabari, part 2, 271.
143 Sahih al-Bukhari, Kitab al-Maghazi, Bab Maradh al-Nabi, 4432. Sahih Muslim, Kitab al-Wasiya, Bab Tark al-Wasiya, 4233, 4234. Tarikh al-Tabari, part 2, 271.

write. Second, he claimed that they already had the Quran, and therefore there was no need for another final letter from Mohammed. Third, he insisted that Mohammed had lost his mind.[144] This was another victory for Abu Bakr.

Nevertheless, after the death of Mohammed,[145] a strong competitor arose, a cousin of Mohammed named Ali ibn Abi Talib. Ali and Mohammed were raised in the same house. Ali was loyal and fought in all the battles. But more importantly, he married Mohammed's daughter, Fatima. In light of this, Abu Bakr wasted no time declaring himself the first caliph with the help of his ally Umar ibn al-Khattab.[146] He felt that after all the sacrifices he had made, he was entitled to be the first caliph.

When the news of the death of Mohammed reached Arabia, the Arabian tribes, who were forced to join Islam, withdrew from it. They refused to pay their dues. But Abu Bakr would have none of this. He would not lose what he had worked so hard to gain. Therefore, he waged war against those tribes, killing those who refused to return to Islam. Dr. Amari adds, "he did this in accordance with the Quran which orders all Muslims to fight all those who do not believe in Mohammed's claims."[147] These wars were called the wars of Ridda (apostasy). Those

[144] Sahih al-Bukhari, Kitab al-Maghazi, Bab Maradh al-Nabi, 4432. Sahih Muslim, Kitab al-Wasiya, Bab Tark al-Wasiya, 4233, 4234. Tarikh al-Tabari, part 2, 271.
[145] Islamic traditions place the death of Mohammed around 632 A.D.
[146] Tarikh al-Tabari, part 2, 278-282.
[147] Rafat Amari, *Islam in Light of History*, 469.

wars consumed almost all his efforts until his death, before which he named his ally, Umar ibn al-Khattab, as his successor.

Later, Umar occupied Jerusalem, around 637 A.D. The first thing Umar did was seek to find where the Jewish temple was. He wanted to verify for himself the story of Mohammed and the accounts of Abu Bakr's visiting the temple. He went to the temple mount but found no temple.[148] That was the legacy of Abu Bakr.

[148] Rafat Amari, *Quran & History*, 374.

Hafsa

Hafsa bint (daughter of) Umar was her name. She was married to Mohammed, one of several wives. She was the daughter of Umar ibn al-Khattab, one of the first disciples of Mohammed from Mecca's era, and more importantly the ally of Abu Bakr. Umar later became the caliph after Abu Bakr, and after he was assassinated, Uthman ibn Affan became the third caliph. Most traditions attribute more influence and significance to Mohammed's wife Aisha bint Abu Bakr. In the long term, however, Hafsa had the greatest influence.

After the death of Mohammed, the whole nation of Islam was busy with war. First, Abu Bakr was involved in the Ridda wars. These wars were vital for the survival of the nation. Abu Bakr died shortly after the conclusion of these wars, but he made sure that Umar, Hafsa's father, became the next caliph. He also was very busy with attacking the Persians and the Byzantine empires. It was only at the end of Umar's rule that the Islamic nation realized that they had ignored their poetry, their writings, their system, and the Quran. They did not have time for any of this before.[149]

It was in the wake of war that many people realized that the Quranic verses were starting to be lost. Mohammed did not write

[149] Ibn Salam Jamhi, *Tabaqat Fuhul al-Shuara'*, 34.

down the Quran. He appointed only four people to officially memorize the Quran. These official memorizers were called al-Hafatha.[150] After all of the wars, many who had memorized the Quran died. One of the four was Abdullah ibn Masud or Ibn Masud as he was often called. Abu Musa al-Ashaari was one who memorized the Quran, though not one of the four official memorizers. He was one of Mohammed's companions. He insisted that Muslims had forgotten two full surahs.[151]

Abu Musa was not the only person providing these troublesome reports, for Zayd ibn Thabet said that surah al-Inaam and surah al-Araf used to be twice as long.[152] One of the official memorizers of the Quran, Ubay ibn Kaab, stated that surah al-Ahzab used to be considerably longer, equal to or longer than surah al-Baqara.[153] And it contained the famous stoning verse that Hafsa's father, Umar, recited repeatedly.[154] Ali ibn Abi Talib recited a surah called Bara'a.[155] Clearly, memorization was not the right way to preserve the Quran. These verses were gone forever. But Hafsa thought she could do something about it:

[150] Sahih al-Bukhari, Kitab Fadha'il al-Quran, Bab al-Qura' min Ashab al-Nabi, 4999.
[151] Suyuti, *Al-Itqan fi Ulum al-Quran*, 471.
[152] Sijistani, *Al-Masahef*, 502-503. Al-Nisa'i, *Sunan al-Kubra*, 1064.
[153] Daniel Amari, *Dawn of Islam*, 181.
[154] Suyuti, *Al-Itqan fi Ulum al-Quran*, 473.
[155] Masudi, *Muruj al-Thahab*, part 2, 228. This surah is not found in the current Quran.

Umru ibn Rafi` said that he used to write a Quran for Hafsa, the mother of the faithful.[156]

Hafsa told him to write it her own way, the way she heard it.[157] This was her own Quran. All Muslim narrators identified it as the Quran of Hafsa.[158] Even al-Hafatha, memorizers of the Quran, recognized that this was Hafsa's own Quran and her own reading.[159] It consisted of a collection of parchments.

At that time, others had made their own copies. Al-Hafatha made their own. Even other wives of Mohammed, such as Aisha, made their own. The Qurans of al-Hafatha and other companions became widespread in the Islamic nation. That was the reason Hafsa was surprised when the caliph Uthman, the successor of her father, asked to borrow her copy. Why would the caliph

---

[156] Muti' Malik, 459. Cf. Sijistani, *Al-Masahef*, 243, 246.
[157] Muti' Malik, 459. Cf. Sijistani, *Al-Masahef*, 243, 246.
[158] These Islamic narrations clearly contradict the narration in Sahih Bukhari that Zayd ibn Thabet was the one who wrote the Quran in the days of Abu Bakr, then it was eventually given to Hafsa. This narration is clearly unhistorical. Abu Bakr was occupied with civil war. He did not have the time to gather the Quran. Furthermore, if Abu Bakr had the copy, he would have already forced it on all. Moreover, the copy of the Quran was not known as Zayd's Quran but Hafsa's Quran in all narrations. Finally, al-Hafatha referred to Hafsa as the one who wrote it. Yusuf ibn Ishaq al-Kindi's testimony cannot be evidence for the authenticity of al-Bukhari's narration. Al-Kindi was most likely dependent on Bukhari's Hadith. For the sake of argument, even if he was an independent source from al-Bukhari, his attestation would be limited merely to the contention that al-Bukhari did not fabricate it. But that issue was not in dispute here. Rather, the question concerned the authenticity of the narration Bukhari received. This narration was clearly fabricated to cover the embarrassment over Hafsa's gathering of the Quran as confirmed by many other narrations.
[159] Sijistani, *Al-Masahef*, 246.

Uthman want her copy? It was her personal copy after all. She was not one of al-Hafatha, memorizers of the Quran. This Quran reflected her recollections only; besides, she was an illiterate woman. If the caliph needed a good copy of the Quran, why not contact one of the al-Hafatha? Therefore, she refused to let Uthman borrow her copy.[160] Uthman, however, "promised her that he would return her Quran to her."[161] Only then did she agree to let him borrow her Quran.

Sometime later, Uthman returned to her the parchments of the Quran. She went over the parchments but was horrified to discover that some of them were missing. Uthman produced a different Quran, and those parchments that were different from Uthman's new recension[162] were burnt.[163] Hafsa then found out that Uthman ordered the burning of all copies of the Quran, including the copies made by al-Hafatha. This was a religious and political coup. Uthman had corrupted the Quran. He had broken his promise to Hafsa and could not be trusted.

The burning of some, if not most, of the parchments of Hafsa explained why Hafsa later rejected Marwan's request. Marwan was a cousin of Uthman whom Uthman appointed as his assistant. He was practically running the affairs of the Islamic state. When he later became the governor of Medina, he

[160] Sijistani, *Al-Masahef*, 30.
[161] Sijistani, *Al-Masahef*, 30.
[162] New version by editing a previous one.
[163] Sahih al-Bukhari, Kitab Fadha'il al-Quran, Bab Jama` al-Quran, 4987. Observe how the narration differentiated between a book and parchments. The term "parchments" is a reference to the collection of parchments of Hafsa.

repeatedly demanded that Hafsa give him her remaining parchments. She utterly rejected his request.[164] But he never gave up. When she died, he barely waited for her funeral to conclude before he demanded the parchments from her brother, Abdullah ibn Umar, who complied. Marwan destroyed the parchments.[165] Abdullah ibn Umar had the following to say about this:

> Let no one say I have received all of the Quran, for he does not know what all of it is. Much of the Quran has been lost. Let him say I received from the Quran only what remained from it.[166]

There is a reason that Marwan demanded the parchments of Hafsa. The Umayyads continued editing the Quran such that the parchments of Hafsa contradicted the newer copies of the Quran. Not only was Hafsa's Quran destroyed, but the original Uthmanic Quran was gone as well.[167]

There was major difference between the early transmission of the Quran and the early transmission of the New Testament. In the 2nd and 3rd centuries, there was no religious entity, such as a caliph, controlling Christianity. In fact, Christians were suffering persecution by the Roman empire. Manuscripts of the New Testament were copied independently and freely. For this reason, textual critics can retrieve over 99% of the original text

---

[164] Sijistani, *Al-Masahef*, 72.
[165] Sijistani, *Al-Masahef*, 30, 73, 85. Balatheri, *Ansab al-Ashraf*, part 2, 60.
[166] Suyuti, *Al-Itqan fi Ulum al-Quran*, 470.
[167] Sijistani, *Al-Masahef*, 119.

of the New Testament with confidence, due to the almost 100 manuscripts of the New Testament that were dated before the 4th century A.D. When compared to later texts, these manuscripts demonstrate fidelity to the earliest (original) versions of the text. On the other hand, the text of the Quran was controlled by Uthman and the rest of the caliphs. They destroyed all the earlier copies of the Quran. As Abdullah ibn Umar perceptively articulated, "Much of the Quran has been lost. Let him say I received from the Quran only what remained from it."[168] In order to conduct effective textual criticism on the Quran, one would first need the manuscripts of the Quran that Uthman burned. Therefore, meaningful textual criticism of the Quran today is not possible.

[168] Suyuti, *Al-Itqan fi Ulum al-Quran*, 470.

Ibn Masud

Abdullah ibn Masud was an important figure in the history of the transmission of the Quran. He was one of the four people (called al-Hafatha) whom Mohammed appointed to memorize the Quran,[169] and he was probably the most important of them. It was interesting how this position of authorized memorizer of the Quran came to be.

Mohammed never cared to write down the verses of the Quran.[170] This led to a major problem because Mohammed was prone to forget the verses of the Quran[171] and thus used to recite contradictory versions of the same verses or surahs.[172] This caused problems among Muslims. To them, these verses were inspired by Allah. To alleviate these problems, Mohammed used various strategies. First, he used threats to discourage Muslims from discussing the differences. He said that Allah caused those who discussed such differences to perish.[173] Second, he blamed

---

[169] Sahih al-Bukhari, Kitab Fadha'il al-Quran, Bab al-Qura' min Ashab al-Nabi, 4999.
[170] Islamic traditions have many direct references that state that Mohammed was not an illiterate. Cf. Rafat Amari, *Quran & History*, 448-460.
[171] Sahih Bukhari, Kitab Fadha'il al-Quran, Bab Nasayan al-Quran.
[172] Sahih Bukhari, Kitab Fadha'il al-Quran, Bab Man lam yara Baasa, 5041.
[173] Sahih Bukhari, Kitab Fadha'il al-Quran, Bab Iqra'u al-Quran ma Iatalafat Aalayhi Qulubukom, 5062.

Allah for the multiple versions and his forgetfulness. In the Quran 2:106:

> Whatever verse we change or cause to be forgotten, we bring another one better than it or like it. Do you not know that Allah can do anything?[174]

Third, Mohammed prohibited Muslims from discussing differing versions. He even ordered them to leave when the subject came up.[175] Evidently, none of these strategies worked. Therefore, Mohammed came up with a fourth strategy. He appointed four Muslims to be the authorized memorizers of the Quran. He introduced them to Muslims and announced that all Muslims should receive the correct version of the Quran from them. In other words, Mohammed did not want to be bothered with any problem regarding verses of the Quran. If anybody had a question or a problem, the problem was for these four people to resolve. The four al-Hafatha were Salem, Muath, Ubay ibn Kaab, and Abdullah ibn Masud.[176]

After Mohammed died, the Islamic world was involved in the Ridda wars, and wars to push into the Persian and the Byzantine empires. The collective memories of these al-Hafatha was not reliable. Many surahs were forgotten.[177] Relying on

[174] Thaalibi, *Al-Jawar al-Husan fi Tafsir al-Quran*, verse 2:106 provides narration that supports the above conclusion.
[175] Sahih Bukhari, Kitab Fadha'il al-Quran, Bab Iqra'u al-Quran ma Iatalafat Aalayhi Qulubukom, 5060.
[176] Sahih al-Bukhari, Kitab Fadha'il al-Quran, Bab al-Qura' min Ashab al-Nabi, 4999.
[177] Cf. the chapter on Hafsa.

memory alone to transmit a text was clearly a failed strategy, but was realized as such only after Mohammed's death. Therefore, al-Hafatha started to write down their versions of the Quran, as did some of Mohammed's companions, such as Ali ibn Abi Talib and Abu Musa al-Ashaari, and some of Mohammed's wives, such as Hafsa and Aisha.[178] This strategy would have succeeded if it had been used during Mohammed's time and supervised by Mohammed. But now it was too late. There were major differences between the various versions of the Quran as surahs were added and omitted from various versions.[179]

It was very understandable that Ibn Masud became furious when Uthman, the caliph, ordered the burning of his version of the Quran in favor of the new Quran edited by Zayd ibn Thabet based on Hafsa's version. Ibn Masud's version was spread mostly in al-Kufa in Iraq. In return, Ibn Masud rebelled. He asked the people of al-Kufa to hide their copies of the Quran, and he blasted Zayd ibn Thabet's credibility and competency. Ibn Masud stated that Zayd was a child and his father was an infidel when he [Ibn Masud] was a Muslim memorizing the Quran.[180]

Ibn Masud continued to make his case. He reminded Muslims that he was one of al-Hafatha, the only group Mohammed authorized to preserve the Quran. He was correct in his assessment. Zayd ibn Thabet was too young to remember all

[178] Al-Suyuti, *Al-Itqan fi Ulum al-Quran*, 130.
[179] Al-Suyuti, *Al-Itqan fi Ulum al-Quran*, 141, 143, 144, 754.
[180] Sijistani, *Al-Masahef*, 51, 63.

the verses, especially the Meccan ones. He was not part of al-Hafatha. Furthermore, there was a clear and intentional effort to exclude al-Hafatha in Uthman's project. Uthman's actions clearly suggested that he was not interested in getting the most accurate Quran, but instead had ulterior motives.

Uthman's response to Ibn Masud was violent. He removed Ibn Masud from his position in al-Kufa and brought him to Medina. He beat him.[181] He imprisoned him.[182] He also imprisoned the only other member of al-Hafatha who was alive, Ubay ibn Kaab.[183] This demonstrated that Uthman's actions were not driven by a personal vendetta against Ibn Masud but rather was aimed against al-Hafatha who criticized the new Quran. On the counsel of Uthman's cousin, Marwan ibn al-Hakam, Uthman prevented Ibn Masud from leaving Medina until his death.[184] All who supported the reading of Ibn Masud faced violent persecution.[185]

The fact that the Quran was not written down by Mohammed is significant. He was the apostle of Islam, and yet he did not care for the Quran. For Mohammed, the Quran was a tool to be used to achieve his personal desires, punish his personal enemies, justify his own deeds, and control the Muslims. By contrast, the apostles of Christ supervised the

[181] Taha Hussein, *Al-Fitna al-Kubra*, Part 1, 160-183. Balathiri, *Ansab al-Ashraf*, Part 5, 525.
[182] Sira al-Halabiyya, Part 2, 108.
[183] Sira al-Halabiyya, Part 2, 108.
[184] Balathiri, *Ansab al-Ashraf*, Part 5, 524-525.
[185] Yaqut al-Hamawi, *Maajam al-Udaba'*, Part 17, 168-169.

writing and the transmission of the New Testament text in the 1st century A.D. Furthermore, beginning immediately after the death of Mohammed, Islam was always controlled by strong caliphs. Uthman's control of the text of the Quran implies we can never textually arrive at the original text of the Quran.

Contrary to the Quran, in the 2nd and the 3rd centuries of Christianity, the most critical centuries for the transmission of the text of the New Testament, there was no Christian caliph who controlled the transmission of the text. And thus the differences between the New Testament manuscripts were preserved, documented, and valued.

Marwan

Marwan was from the famous Meccan tribe Banu Abd-Shams (the slaves of the sun). His father was al-Hakam ibn Abu al-Aas. His great grandfather was Umayya. His cousin was Uthman, who became the third Caliph. Abu Sufyan was a grandchild of Umayya. This family from the line of Umayya son of Abd Shams became the Umayyad dynasty. This is their story.

Marwan and especially his father, al-Hakam, were not fond of Mohammed. When Uthman became a Muslim, his uncle, al-Hakam, warned him that he could not be loyal to both his tribe and his new religion.[186] In a sense, Uthman always felt that he owed his family loyalty. He thought highly of his cousin Marwan.

Marwan saw the humiliation of his family. He saw how badly Abu Sufyan was treated. But then it was his father's turn to face Mohammed's judgment. Al-Hakam was never convinced of the truth of Islam. Now he found himself forced to become a Muslim in exchange for his life. The only thing he was able to do was to make mocking faces while Mohammed prayed. He made sure to sit behind Mohammed so he would not be seen by him.[187] Normally, this would be a capital offense. Any person

---

[186] Balathiri, *Ansab al-Ashraf*, Part 5, 481.
[187] Ibn Manthur, *Lisan al-Arab*, Bab al-Kha', Khalaj, 1223.

who said anything bad about Mohammed would be slaughtered by the orders of Mohammed. But probably because of Uthman, Mohammed opted to exile al-Hakam to the city of Ta'if.[188]

For Marwan, sending his father to exile was very difficult. From his perspective, Mohammed was the aggressor and his father was the victim. But it affected Uthman as well. The following narration captures their perspective: After Mohammed died and Abu Bakr became the caliph, Uthman approached him to bring his uncle back from exile. Abu Bakr refused. Uthman protested, "but he is my uncle." Abu Bakr replied, "your uncle is in hell. I will never change anything that the apostle of Allah did. I will never bring him back." But Uthman did not give up. After Abu Bakr died and Umar became the caliph, Uthman approached him concerning the same issue. But Umar said to him, "Woe to you, Uthman, you are speaking of the one who was cursed and kicked out by the apostle of Allah, the enemy of the Allah and the enemy of his apostle."[189]

This insightful narration suggests that Uthman held two loyalties—one to Islam and the other to his Umayyad tribe. The time would come for Uthman to favor one over the other. Umar was assassinated.[190] Uthman became the caliph.[191] Of course one of the first things he did was bring his uncle, al-Hakam, back

[188] Tarikh al-Tabari, Part 5, 685.
[189] Sira al-Halabiyya, Part 2, 105.
[190] Around 644 A.D.
[191] There was tension and threat of violence in Uthman's choice of verses against Ali ibn Abi Talib. Ali seemed to have been forced to support Uthman as a caliph. Cf. Balathiri, *Ansab al-Ashraf*, Part 5, 507-508.

from exile.[192] He replaced various governors and filled other important positions with people from his own tribe.[193] Specifically, he appointed the son of Abu Sufyan, Muawiya, as the governor of Damascus.[194] Uthman used public money to generously reward his tribe members,[195] and in particular Marwan[196] and his brother.[197]

Uthman appointed Marwan as his clerk.[198] The truth is that he was his counselor, effectively running the affairs of the state.[199] The Umayyads were now back in control. Uthman was truly the first Umayyad caliph, as Patricia Crone and Martin Hinds explain.[200] One would wonder what they would do with Islam, which was forced upon them. Instead of coming forward with the truth about Islam, they calculated that it was more important for them to propagate Islam to maintain their power. This required major theological changes in the Islamic state.

The position of caliph needed to be elevated so that he would be the source of authority. For the first time, caliph of Uthman was given the title "caliph of Allah" meaning the

---

192 Sira al-Halabiyya, Part 2, 105. Masudi, *Muruj al-Thahab*, Part 3, 149.
193 Sira al-Halabiyya, Part 2, 105.
194 Masudi, *Muruj al-Thahab*, Part 2, 263.
195 Tarikh al-Tabari, Part 2, 745.
196 Balathiri, *Ansab al-Ashraf*, Part 5, 514. Sira al-Halabiyya, Part 2, 108. Tarikh al-Tabari, Part 2, 704.
197 Balathiri, *Ansab al-Ashraf*, Part 5, 515. Sira al-Halabiyya, Part 2, 108.
198 Tarikh al-Tabari, Part 3, 581.
199 Tarikh al-Tabari, Part 2, 754.
200 Patricia Crone, Martin Hinds, *God's Caliph* (Cambridge University Press, 2003), 32.

"deputy of Allah."[201] This title was adopted by nearly all the Umayyad caliphs.[202] In contrast, Abu Bakr and Umar were referred to by the title of the caliphs of the Apostle of Allah,[203] a modest title that expressed dependency on the authority of Mohammed as the prophet.[204] For the Umayyads now, the concept of caliph was not as dependent on Mohammed as it was on the fact that Uthman, and later the Umayyad dynasty, were chosen by Allah just as Mohammed was chosen by Allah.[205] In other words, it was not the tribe of Mohammed who should rule, but the tribe of Uthman, the Umayyads. Clearly, this concept developed later, but the fact that this title was applied to Uthman suggests that the Umayyads initiated this theological change. The Quran, however, was an obstacle.

First, the Quran contained verses that favored the family of Mohammed. These verses had been used by Ali ibn Abi-Talib to highlight the fact that he was Mohammed's cousin and married to his daughter Fatima. These verses needed to be omitted.[206]

Second, as Dr. Rafat Amari states, "Muslims in those times did not accept application of any law or legislation that was not derived from the Quran."[207] Therefore, verses needed to be added to the Quran. The Umayyads pursued exactly the same

[201] Crone, Hinds, *God's Caliph*, 5-6.
[202] Crone, Hinds, *God's Caliph*, 6-11.
[203] Crone, Hinds, *God's Caliph*, 19-20.
[204] Crone, Hinds, *God's Caliph*, 22.
[205] Crone, Hinds, *God's Caliph*, 31-32.
[206] Rafat Amari, *Quran & History*, 372.
[207] Rafat Amari, *Quran & History*, 371.

strategy of Mohammed of utilizing the Quran as a tool to control Muslims. The Umayyads needed a religious text, and Muslims looked up to the Quran.

Third, when he was caliph, Umar had occupied Christian nations that were far more developed theologically, historically, and scientifically. The current Quran was not appropriate for these nations. Dr. Rafat Amari explains:

> The Quran came under scrutiny and criticism by Christians. This induced the Umayyad caliph to edit the Quran and omit the things which were mostly criticized. They added some verses that alleviated from the gravity of other verses that had mythological character or illogical meanings. Such as the fifth verse of surah 32 called As-Sajda, which made the distance between earth and heaven as one thousand years walk. The Umayyad added another verse: the fourth verse of Surah Al-Maarij (number 70), which made the distance to be 50 thousand years walk.[208]

The Christian concept of monotheism was far superior to the one that Mohammed preached. Mohammed preached that Allah was Venus and that his wife and daughters were to be honored. There was an explicit verse in surah al-Najm (the star) that advocated direct worship of Allat, Uzza, and Manat.[209] The polytheism of the Quran needed to be toned down, monotheistic slogans needed to be emphasized, and Unitarianism needed to be presented as true monotheism.[210]

[208] Rafat Amari, *Quran & History*, 371.
[209] Daniel Amari, *Dawn of Islam,* 187.
[210] Daniel Amari, *Dawn of Islam,* 187.

A major recension of the Quran was needed. This was the most important project Marwan undertook under the name of the caliph Uthman. If Marwan, and the Umayyads, had truly wanted to compile or gather a version of the Quran that represented the most accurate and faithful transmission of the verses of the Quran by Mohammed, they would have created a committee that consisted of al-Hafatha of the Quran. The committee would have included Ibn Masud, Ubay ibn Kaab, Abu Musa al-Ashaari, Ali ibn Abi Talib, and others.[211] All of the copies of the Quran would be consulted including the ones by Ali ibn Abi Talib, Ibn Abbas, Abu Musa al-Ashaari, and many others. All these earlier copies would have been preserved as the treasure of the Islamic state and protected at any cost. They would be more sacred than the temple of Kaaba itself.[212]

Given the fact that the true purpose of the project was neither to gather the Quran, nor to compile it, nor to produce the most authentic Quran of Mohammed,[213] but rather to produce a new version of the Quran, the following was needed. First, a low-profile personal copy of the Quran. This explained the interest in Hafsa's Quran. Second, al-Hafatha had to be excluded and controlled. Third, an editorial team was needed to add and delete verses. This effort was led by Zayd ibn Thabet. Fourth, a linguistic team was needed to fix the errors and the stylistic

[211] Salem and Muath were dead by that time.
[212] Apparently, the Umayyads did not respect Kaaba nor Mecca as we will demonstrate in the next chapter.
[213] As we have seen in previous chapter, this was not possible given that Mohammed did not write down the Quran.

weakness of Hafsa. This was led by Said ibn al-Aas.[214] Finally, they needed to act swiftly and collect all other versions and destroy them, and this is exactly what happened.

Rewriting the Quran was a very bold move. It did not go unnoticed. Muslims were outraged over this. They explicitly stated their reasons, such as, "we are angry because [Uthman] wiped out the book of Allah." [215] Understandably, these accusations were repeated by many Muslims as their main concern against Uthman. Muslims knew that Marwan was behind this. One of the greatest critics of this revision was Ali ibn Abi-Talib. He met Uthman and strongly denounced Marwan. [216] The Umayyads, however, strongly defended Uthman and Marwan and accused Ali of causing revolt and unrest. [217] Finally, an angry mob surrounded Uthman and demanded the blood of Marwan, but Uthman refused. [218] Uthman probably remembered the words of his uncle, al-Hakam, the father of Marwan, about making a choice.[219] This time he paid for his loyalty to his tribe with his life. Uthman was assassinated. Muslims were so angry at him that they kept his body from being buried for three days.[220]

This was the start of a series of civil wars between Ali ibn Abi-Talib, who declared himself a caliph, and the Umayyads led

[214] Sahih al-Bukhari, Kitab Fadha'il al-Quran, Bab Jama` al-Quran, 4987.
[215] Sijistani, *Al-Masahef*, 121.
[216] Tarikh al-Tabari, Part 2, 754.
[217] Tarikh al-Tabari, Part 2, 756.
[218] Sira al-Halabiyya, Part 2, 106-107.
[219] Balathiri, *Ansab al-Ashraf*, Part 5, 481.
[220] Sira al-Halabiyya, Part 2, 105.

by the son of Abu Sufyan, Muawiya, who later declared himself a caliph as well. Ali was assassinated and Muawiya ibn Abu Sufyan won the first war. He appointed Marwan the governor of Medina.

Marwan went after the remaining Quranic parchments of Hafsa and continued his project of editing the Quran. Dr. Rafat Amari explains:

> Though the Umayyad's policy was to gather the copies of Quran under the excuse of editing them, they came up with new copies of Quran; the Quran of Hafsa, however, which was returned to her after it was edited, was a hindrance before the Umayyads in their plan of developing the Quran. Many Muslims returned to the copy of Hafsa in order to judge the differences of the verses.[221]

Division, civil wars, and assassinations continued in Islam, on account of the corruption of the Quran. Hasan, one of the sons of Ali, was poisoned. Hussein, his other son, took over the resistance. Hussein was famous for stating, "I believe in what was omitted from the Quran, and I blaspheme (disbelief) those verses that were added to it."[222] This is because the original verses that sympathized with the family of Mohammed, Ali, and by implication his children, were removed. Later Hussein was killed.

[221] Rafat Amari, *Quran & History*, 371-372.
[222] Ibn Shahr Ashub, *Mutashabeh al-Quran wa-Mukhtalifeh*, Part 2, 77.

After Muawiya, then Yazid his son, and the abdication of Muawiya II, Marwan became the caliph.[223] There was much work to be completed. First, the Quran needed to be edited further. Second, a competitor named Abdullah ibn Zubayr also declared himself a caliph. Although Marwan did not rule for long, he at least made sure that Abd al-Malek, his son, would succeed him. This was the start of the Marwanid Dynasty, a branch of the Umayyads, whose reign would last for a relatively long time.

[223] Around 684 A.D.

Al-Hajjaj

Uthman ibn Affan had key people to help him. Marwan helped him with running the state. Zayd ibn Thabet was his editor of the Quran. Said ibn al-Aas was his linguistic expert. When Abd al-Malek ibn Marwan became the Umayyad caliph,[224] he faced challenges similar to, if not greater than, the challenges Uthman faced. There was a civil war with another competitor caliph in the province of al-Hijaz, Abdullah ibn Zubayr. Al-Hijaz was a significant province since it included the cities of Mecca and Medina. Furthermore, the Quran needed further editing. Whereas Uthman had Marwan, Zayd, and Said as an editing team, Abd al-Malek had a single editor, al-Hajjaj ibn Yousef al-Thaqafi. As Marwan ran the affairs of the state for Uthman, so al-Hajjaj did the same for Abd al-Malek.

Al-Hajjaj was a shrewd military general, a cunning politician,[225] a devout loyalist, and a capable editor and top linguist. It would be hard to believe in the existence of such a person if not for the definite historical evidence of him, such as coins bearing his name. As a military general, he attacked Mecca, destroyed Kaaba,[226] and killed the caliph Abdullah ibn

[224] Around 685 A.D.
[225] Balathiri, *Ansab al-Ashraf*, Part 13, 399.
[226] Sira al-Halabiyya, Part 1, 231,258.

Zubayr, the competitor of Abd al-Malek.[227] As a cunning and harsh politician,[228] he was able to subdue the city of Kufa and other cities in Iraq. He married the granddaughter of Ali ibn Abi-Talib, but Abd al-Malek ordered him to divorce her, and he did.[229] He was the first to mint Islamic coins for the Islamic nation. He wrote his name on them since he was appointed the governor of al-Hijaz.[230] He was an eloquent linguist.[231] In his day, there were advancements in the quality of Arabic writing.[232] Abd al-Malek ordered the translations of works into Arabic, and al-Hajjaj personally oversaw these translation projects.[233]

Al-Hajjaj served two caliphs. When Abd al-Malek died around 705 A.D., al-Walid took over. Al-Walid continued to depend on al-Hajjaj as well. One thing to note is that during the era of al-Walid, Ali the son of Hussein son of Ali ibn Abi-Talib was assassinated. Ali and his descendants were always the target of assassination. Al-Hajjaj achieved many accomplishments for both Abd al-Malek and al-Walid. His most important accomplishment, however, was editing the Quran. His work marks an important recension of the Quran.

---

[227] Sira al-Halabiyya, Part 1, 258.
[228] Sira al-Halabiyya, Part 1, 261.
[229] Ibn Hazm Andulusi, *Jamharat Ansab al-Arab*, Part 1, 68.
[230] Sira al-Halabiyya, Part 1, 262. Compare with Tarikh ibn Khaldoun, volume 1, 323.
[231] Asqalani, *Tahthib al-Tahthib*, letter ha, 363.
[232] Tarikh ibn Khaldoun, volume 1, 303.
[233] Tarikh ibn Khaldoun, volume 1, 303.

What was the justification for editing the Quran? It was the same justification that Uthman used: gathering the Quran.[234] Clearly, Hafsa gathered the Quran. Gathering the Quran was a term used by Uthman and Abd al-Malek for intentional editing of the Quran for the purpose of creating a new version.

This brings us to the question of the justification for modifying the Quran. For the Umayyads, the caliph was neither subservient nor inferior to Mohammed. For al-Hajjaj, the caliph Abd al-Malek was greater than Mohammed, as explicitly stated by al-Hajjaj.[235] For the Umayyads, Mohammed set a very low bar. The fact that they were Muslims did not change the truth that their tribe was never convinced of Mohammed and that they had been forced to become Muslims. They did not see anything in Mohammed that merited his being called a prophet.

Even now, as al-Hajjaj looked at the Quran, he felt that he was superior linguistically. In fact, if Abd al-Malek was greater than Mohammed, why would divine inspiration (al-Wahi) that inspired the Quran be exclusive only to Mohammed? It would not be, according to al-Hajjaj, who insisted that he did everything with divine inspiration (al-Wahi), as the following narration illustrates:

[234] Ibn Athir, *Al-Kamel fi al-Tarikh*, Part 4, 237.
[235] Balathiri, *Ansab al-Ashraf*, Part 13, 379.

> When the prophet died, Um Ayman [the mother of Ayman] started to cry, and she will not stop crying. Abu Bakr told Umar, "let us visit that woman." They entered her home and said, "O Um Ayman, why are you crying? The apostle of Allah has gone to what is better for him than this world." She replied, "I am not crying for this reason. I know that he went to what is better for him than this world. But I am crying because of the divine inspiration [meaning al-Wahi that gives the Quran] has stopped." When this narration was reported to al-Hajjaj, he said, "Um Ayman lied. Nothing that I do is without the divine inspiration [al-Wahi]."[236]

The context of the divine inspiration referred to in the above quotation is the inspiration of the Quran. Furthermore, al-Hajjaj had the utmost contempt for versions prior to his own.[237] He thought that his new version was superior. He would kill any person who questioned his religious rituals even if they contradicted Mohammed.[238]

Then what did al-Hajjaj change? Or, a better question: what were the changes during his lifetime? First, he modified the Quran linguistically. Kitab al-Masahef mentions several examples.[239] Based on my research on the manuscripts of the Quran, I found clear attestation to some of the changes that were attributed to al-Hajjaj or his era. The manuscript evidence, however, suggests that the changes were widespread and

---

[236] Ibn Asaker, *Tarikh Madinat Dimashq*, Part 12, 160. Cf. Balathiri, *Ansab al-Ashraf*, Part 13, 363.
[237] Balathiri, *Ansab al-Ashraf*, Part 13, 386. Cf. Balathiri, *Ansab al-Ashraf*, part 13, 387.
[238] Balathiri, *Ansab al-Ashraf*, Part 13, 366.
[239] Sijistani, *Al-Masahef*, 142, 347.

overarching. [240] The changes that the Islamic traditions mentioned were only a tiny fraction of the modifications made to the Quran in history. Furthermore, these reports of alterations, whether they were additions, omissions, or modifications, are historical. In addition, various changes were made to the organization of the Quran such as the partition, naming, and order of the surahs.[241]

Second, verses were added to the Quran such as Quran 17:1:

> Praise be to the one who took his servant on a night journey from Masjid al-Haram [Mecca Mosque] to Masjid al-Aqsa [Masjid al-Aqsa in Jerusalem on the temple mount] which we have blessed around it, in order to show him [Mohammed] from our signs [miracles]. For he is hearing and seeing.

During the civil war with the caliph Abdullah ibn Zubayr, who controlled Mecca, the Umayyads, who were stationed in Damascus and controlled Jerusalem, found it politically expedient to change the location of Hajj from Mecca to Jerusalem. Therefore, the caliph Abd al-Malek built the Aqsa Mosque around 691 A.D.[242] Dr. Rafat Amari concludes:

> We can only conclude that surah 17:1 was added later than 691 A.D., long after the construction of the mosque called Masjid al-Aqsa.

[240] Daniel Amari, *Dawn of Islam,* 207.
[241] Sijistani, *Al-Masahef*, 354. Asqalani, *Tahthib al-Tahthib*, 364.
[242] Rafat Amari, *Quran & History*, 373.

Obviously, the editor made a historical error. He should have added the term that Mohammed used, Bayt al-Maqdis, instead of Aqsa Mosque. At the same time, the Umayyads needed to add support for the actual name of that Masjid.[243] No doubt, earlier commentaries on the Quran (Tafsir) accepted as a fact that al-Hajjaj had modified the Quran.[244]

Shortly after al-Hajjaj died, the caliph al-Walid died as well. The Umayyads, however, and the Marwanids in particular, remained in power until 750 A.D. The Abbasids dynasty, the descendants of Abbas, the uncle of Mohammed, took over after slaughtering the remnants of the Umayyads. The exception was Andalusia (Spain) where the Umayyads continued to rule.

The principle that the words of God need to be preserved and not to be added to or modified is a biblical one. It was not an early Islamic principle—and certainly not the understanding of the Umayyad caliphs. Only later did Islam adopt this principle from Christianity. The clerics, in their attempt to deflect the amount of corruption that beset the Quran, have claimed that the Bible was corrupted. Yet, in centuries of Islamic traditions, none was able to provide evidence to support this claim. In modern times, we have moved beyond the simple fact that we can arrive at over 99% of the original text of the Bible. Investigation of the

[243] The modern suggestion that this was a different mosque cannot be taken seriously, for it stands in opposition to the totality of Islamic traditions. This modern suggestion is nothing but an apologetical attempt that has no place in credible historical investigation. For further detailed discussion about this, cf. Dr. Rafat Amari, *Quran & History*, chapter of al-Isra', 371-390.

[244] Ibn Hayyan, *Al-Bahr al-Muhit*, Part 17, 453; commentary on verse 34:31.

habits of the scribes of the Bible shows that they copied the text faithfully with the intention of preserving the text and not corrupting it.[245]

[245]Phillip M. Miller, "The Least Orthodox Reading is to be Preferred: A New Canon for New Testament Textual Criticism?" in *Revisiting the Corruption of the New Testament: Manuscript, Patristic, and Apocryphal Evidence, ed.* Daniel B. Wallace (Grand Rapids: Kregel Publications, 2011), 89.

Sufism[246]

During the Abbasid rule, a movement was born as a religious rebellion against the political minded system of Islam. The history of Islam thus far had been about wars, killings, assassinations, power struggles, and competing caliphs. The movement known as Sufism was based on the Arabic word suf (wool). It initially sought within the rituals of Islam the religiosity that a religion ought to embody. Therefore, the initial form of this movement was to follow the Islamic rituals, to find spiritual meaning from the Islamic practices of prayer, fasting, and others. It differentiated itself by the fact that it tried to imitate the monks of other religions in their monastic practices and even their clothes, and hence their name was derived from "wool."

Apparently, this initial endeavor did not achieve its goals. For theologically, Islam was built around the caliph and the nation. The Quran, Islamic tradition, and Islamic practices were built to support that sociopolitical system. In addition, the concept of deity in Islam was not one that induced love. As early as the 8th century A.D., the Islamic concept of deity had evolved to unitarian monotheism. If the ultimate expression of

[246] This brief article is taken from a larger work by Daniel Amari titled *Sufism*.

spirituality and religion is love, then where is love in Allah? Before Allah created the universe and the angels, who did he love and who admired him? This is the most powerful argument against unitarian monotheism. Islam, therefore, did not offer the desired answer for a religious-centric system. There needed to be another system, foreign to Islam that provided the religious system at the expense of monotheism.

Contrary to Islam, Christianity's concept of monotheism is Trinitarianism. God, before creating the world, always existed as one God but in three persons. These eternal persons were in eternal loving relationships with each other. This is the reason that love is the essence of the concept of deity in Christianity. It is possible that Sufism began to seek love as a reaction to this Christian model of divine love.

Sufism, however, sought its spirituality through the emanationistic panentheism of Neoplatonism. Pantheism is the belief that God is everything. Panentheism is the belief that God is *in* everything. In particular, God is behind the visible things of this world. Emanationistic panentheism refers to the idea that everything in the invisible world and in the spiritual world was emanated from the one deity. In that system, the souls of humans emanated from the "one." Therefore, in this system, the souls of humans are eternal. This provided the missing link. God is loving because God was able to love and be loved by the eternal souls of humans that emanated from him.

Clearly, this is not Islam, but the movement strongly insisted that it is. There was no doubt that any deserters of Islam would be killed; therefore, Sufism strongly utilized monotheistic slogans. This did not prevent the persecution of its members in history. The famous Sufi Al-Hallaj, for instance, was executed for stating that he was the truth and he was Allah. This is no different from early Islam's preaching monotheism while in practice it was henotheism.[247] Likewise, this movement was truly panentheistic with monotheistic slogans. How did it reconcile the two positions? It claimed that Islam with its sacred texts of Quran and Hadith was the religion of the visible world. So for the visible world, they are devout Muslims. The Quran, however, is not appropriate for the invisible world, nor is salvation found in the visible or apparent religion. One must have the courage to abandon the visible religion to go deeper to the true religion and connect to the deity who is everything in the invisible world.

How did that movement achieve its connection? Through occultism. There are certain practices that are meant to send the practitioner into a state of unconsciousness. It is in that state that one achieves connection with the invisible self and therefore with god. The practitioner then returns after being indwelled with the spiritual entities, demons, encountered in the state of unconsciousness. In a sense, in its practices Sufism is the return to the predecessor of Islam, the religion of Jinn.

Neoplatonism, a modified version of Platonism, was a philosophical response to Christianity, and yet Neoplatonism

[247] A religious system that preaches monotheism while practicing polytheism due to its polytheistic roots.

failed in love. Sufism, in adopting Neoplatonism, became a mystical branch of Islam. It sought to address the problem of lack of love in the Islamic deity. But this attempt is not without fundamental problems. It fails to provide convincing answers to the following questions: Did God learn love only after he created the physical world and the souls who could return love to him? Is this not a refutation of the perfection of God that demands that he love and be loved eternally? And if Neoplatonism responds with the eternity of the human souls, are these love poems generated from these souls also eternal or were they realized only after these souls were united with their physical bodies after creation? Where is the loving relationship when God creates a mirror that reflects love for him from one direction, i.e., from the direction of creatures to him?

Bridge to Modern Islam

No doubt this version of Islam is not the one familiar to most readers. Islam has evolved. But the modern version of Islam is not identical to what Mohammed preached.

Concerning the concept of deity in Islam, sometime in the 7th century A.D. a debate occurred among the followers of Islam. The idea that Allah was a star, among other primitive concepts, was not well received by the more advanced nations. Influenced by Christian theology, Muslims modified the concept of deity in Islam to a form of monotheism compatible with their pagan roots. Whenever paganism borrowed from biblical concepts, it followed a predictable pattern: It copied monotheism, it copied some elements of transcendental qualities of God, but it failed to understand the doctrine of the Trinity. This is exactly what began to happen in the 7th century A.D. after the death of Mohammed of course.

Furthermore, the Arabic term Allah started to take upon itself a generic attribute. Probably in the early 8th^{h} century A.D. some started to use this term as a generic term for god in Arabic. This was likely first observed by those nations and tribes whose native language was not Arabic, but it was forced upon them. This phenomenon is consistent with all external evidence and Arabic translations. Therefore, it is vital not to formulate the early doctrine of Islamic deity based on Christian Arabs' late usage of the term Allah.

The same development happened to the Quran. Muslim caliphs and clerics have found it difficult to continue to modify the Quran. First, it was impractical to locate all the versions of the Quran, recall them, and replace them. Moreover, that practice was heavily criticized by Christians. For Christians, the preservation of scripture is vital. The idea of preservation of sacred text was not embraced by early Muslims but was a later concept. The Islamic claim that the Christian scriptures were corrupted is merely a reaction and a defense mechanism against Christians' pointing out that the caliphs were substantially modifying the Quran.

Reminiscent of what the caliphs have done to the Quran in history, in 1924 in Cairo, Egypt, several clerics examined differing versions of the Quran, selected one of them, and presented it to the Muslims of the world as the perfect copy of the Quran that was never modified—or so they claimed. With that version, called Hafs, no real data was presented such as the total number of other manuscripts consulted, detailed differences between them, and the technical justification for choosing that version. Instead, Muslim clerics attributed the selection of that version to predestination by Allah.

Today, there is no meaningful response from Muslim clerics to the earliest manuscripts of the Quran that show major differences. More troubling, however, is the fact that there is no attempt at all to produce new versions of the Quran that better reflect such manuscripts. Despite what was done in Egypt concerning Hafs, still today there are differing versions of the Quran circulating in the Islamic world.

Much more can be written about the evolution of Islam. When Christians are challenged about Christianity, they appeal to the life and teachings of Christ as found in Scripture. On the other hand, when Muslim clerics are likewise challenged about Islam, they do not appeal to the true historical version of early Islam. They cannot. They appeal to a later narrative based on a theological construct that was neither taught nor practiced by Mohammed. But that later construct is not the version embraced and taught by the founder, Mohammed. For any meaningful, candid, and thoughtful dialog with Muslims to occur, it must be based on the true and original version of Islam embraced by its founder.

Bibliography

Alusi. *Rouh al-Maani.* Beirut: Dar Ihya' al-Turath al-Arabi.

Amari, Daniel. *John's Logos.* Religion Research Institute, 2019.

__________. *Dawn of Islam.* Religion Research Institute, 2020.

__________. *Sufism.* Religion Research Institute, 2021.

Amari, Rafat. *Quran & History.* Religion Research Institute, 2018.

__________. *Islam in Light of History.* Religion Research Institute, 2004.

__________. *Star Akbar: The History of Allah*, vol. 1. *Religion Research Institute*, 2021.

Andulusi, Ibn Hazm. *Jamharat Ansab al-Arab.* Cairo: Dar al-Maarif.

Ashub, Ibn Shahr. *Mutashabeh al-Quran wa-Mukhtalifeh.* Intisharat Bidar.

Asqalani. *Fath al-Bari.* Al-Salafiyya Bookshop.

__________. *Taththib al-Tahthib.* Maktabat al-Risala, 1995.

Balatheri. *Ansab al-Ashraf.* Beirut: Dar al-Fikr, 1996.

Bukhari. *Sahih al-Bukhari.* Beirut: Al-Asriyya Bookshop, 2008.

Crone, Patricia, & Hinds, Martin. *God's Caliph.* Cambridge University Press, 2003.

Hakem, *Al-Mustadrik ala al-Saheehayn.* Beirut: Dar al-Kotob al-Ilmiya, 2002.

Hamawi, Yaqut. *Maajam al-Udaba'.* Dar al-Ma'mun.

Halabi. *Sira al-Halabiyya.* Beirut: Dar al-Kotob al-Ilmiya, 2013.

Hilali, Asma. *The Sanaa Palimpsest: The transmission of the Quran in the first centuries AH.* Oxford, 2017.

Hussein, Taha. *Al-Fitna al-Kubra.* Cairo: Dar al-Maarif, 2007.

Ibn Anas, Malik. Al-*Muti'.* Abu Dhabi: The Zayed Charitable Foundation, 2004.

Ibn Asaker. *Tarikh Madinat Dimashq.* Beirut: Dar al-Fikr, 1996.

Ibn Athir. *Al-Kamel fi al-Tarikh.* Beirut: Dar al-Kotob al-Ilmiya, 1987.

_______. *Al-Nihaya fi Gharib al-Hadith wa al-Athar.* Dar Ibn al-Juzi, 2000.

Ibn Hanbal. *Musnad Ahmad.* Beirut: Dar al-Kotob al-Ilmiya, 2008.

Ibn Hayyan. *Al-Bahr al-Muhit.* Dar al-Resalah al-Aalamiyya, 2015.

Ibn Hisham. *Sirat ibn Hisham.* Cairo: Dar ibn al-Juzi, 2013.

Ibn Kathir, *Tafsir al-Quran al-Karim.* Beirut: Dar ibn Hazm, 2000.

Ibn Khaldoun. *Tarikh ibn Khaldoun.* Beirut: Dar al-Fikr, 2001.

Ibn Manthur. *Lisan al-Arab.* Cairo: Dar al-Maarif.

Ibn Shahbah, Mohammed. *Al-Israiliyat wa al-Mawduat fi Kutub al-Tafsir.* Cairo: El-Sonna Bookshop, 1987.

Jamhi, Ibn Salam. *Tabaqat Fuhul al-Shuara'.* Dar al-Kotob al-Ilmiya, 2001.

Kalbi. *Kitab al-Asnam.* Cairo: Dar al-Kutub al-Masriyya, 1995.

Kalini. *Al-Kafi.* Beirut: Al-Fajr Publications, 2007.

Masudi. *Muruj al-Thahab.* Beirut: Al-Asriyya Bookshop, 2005.

Miller, Philip M. "The Least Orthodox Reading is to be Preferred: A New Canon for New Testament Textual Criticism?" In *Revisiting the Corruption of the New Testament: Manuscript, Patristic, and Apocryphal Evidence,* edited by Daniel B. Wallace, 57-89. Grand Rapids: Kregel, 2011.

Muslim, *Sahih Muslim.* Beirut: Al-Asriyya Bookshop, 2016.

Nisa'i. *Sunan al-Kubra.* Beirut: Resalah Publishers, 2001.

Qurtubi, *Al-Jame' liAhkam al-Quran.* Beirut: Resalah Publishers, 2006.

Razi. *Mafatih al-Ghayb: Al-Tafsir al-Kabir.* Beirut: Dar al-Fikr, 1981.

Saduq, *Thawab al-Aamal.* Manshurat al-Sherif Radi, 1949.

Sijistani. *Al-Masahef.* Beirut: Dar al-Bashair al-Islamiyya, 2002.

Sulayman, Jamil. *Taalu ila Kalima Sawa'.*

Suyuti. *Al-Itqan fi Ulum al-Quran.* Beirut: Resalah Publishers, 2008.

Tabari. *Jami' al-Bayan fi Tafsir al-Quran.* Beirut: Resalah Publishers, 1994.

________. *Tarikh al-Tabari.* Cairo: Al-Tawfikiya Bookshop, 2016.

Thaalibi. *Al-Jawar al-Husan fi Tafsir al-Quran.* Beirut: Dar Ihya' al-Turath al-Arabi, 1997.

Wahidi. *Asbab Nuzul al-Quran.* Dar al-Kotob al-Ilmiya, 1991.

Zubeidi. *Taj al-Arus.* Kuwait: Al-Turath al-Arabi, 1998.

General Index

Manufactured by Amazon.ca
Bolton, ON

27042262R00072